CW01019641

HOW TO RUN YOUR HOME WITHOUT HELP

Persephone Book Nº 62
Published by Persephone Books Ltd 2005
Reprinted 2014
First published 1949
by John Lehmann

Endpapers taken from 'Riverside',
a 1946 printed dress fabric in rayon crêpe by the
Calico Printers Association

Typeset in ITC Baskerville by Keystroke,
Wolverhampton

Colour by Banbury Litho

Printed and bound in Germany by
GGP Media GmbH, Poessneck

ISBN 978 1 903155 523

Persephone Books Ltd
59 Lamb's Conduit Street
London WC1N 3NB
020 7242 9292

www.persephonebooks.co.uk

HOW TO RUN YOUR HOME WITHOUT HELP

by

KAY SMALLSHAW

****

with a new preface by

CHRISTINA HARDYMENT

PERSEPHONE BOOKS
LONDON

PREFACE

****

When Kay Smallshaw published *How to Run your Home without Help* in 1949, Britain was still recovering from the economic and emotional turmoil of the Second World War. Domestically, it was a push-me-pull-you age, which looked nostalgically backward to the old niceties of home-making, but also longingly forward to a new and democratic world in which efficient domestic technology would enable women to take a much greater part in national life. Although the relationships between men and women had superficially reverted to conventional type, breadwinners and efficient little homebodies, there was yeast in the air, and it was not coming from ovens full of homemade bread.

Life was improving for working-class women. Piped water, the National Grid, improvements in housing, the welfare provisions of the Beveridge report and family allowances, paid directly to mothers, all contributed to their rising standard of living. But for middle-class housewives, these were uniquely hard times. Lives that had been relatively leisured between the wars were now hectic with housekeeping ('the woman of today must be both mistress and maid') thanks to the wartime exodus from domestic service; and it was difficult to keep up appearances at a time when their husband's income was being hard hit by income tax. The labour-saving devices much-trumpeted as effective substitutes for servants were of limited efficiency, and in the case of the washing machine brought a domestic chore once universally farmed out to laundries and washerwomen back into the home.

Kay Smallshaw's advice manual illuminates all these social trends. It gives us a densely-woven background tapestry of the 'domestic spider threads' that plague so many of the heroines of the women's novels published by Persephone Books and offers an enthrallingly detailed picture of their duties: laundering techniques 'from whites to smalls', tips on dealing with recalcitrant coal and gas ranges, methods of darning, bottling fruit, scouring pans and managing children's tea-parties. Reading about the relentless cleaning and polishing, we can understand why, in Dorothy Whipple's 1953 novel *Someone at a Distance,* her heroine Ellen's hands were 'as hard as cuttle-fish' from doing so much of the housework herself.

Although Smallshaw pays lip service to the idea that the housewife must reserve some time for herself every day, she is uncompromising on the keeping up of standards, and envisages an immaculately maintained house, which is both cleaned on a daily basis and deep-cleaned on occasion. 'Daily attentions only scratch the surface of the real house-cleaning that must be done if even a small house or flat is not to get a horrid, neglected look.' Her instructions as to how to fill the unforgiving minute with 60 seconds of good domestic distance run are exhausting to read. The housewife's regular round began before breakfast and included cleaning out coal fires,

****

polishing furniture, brass and silver, doing the washing with only the most basic machine, shopping with a strict eye to 'points', budget and vitamins, and cooking twice a day for the family. And, of course, the mending.

> That mending! When you're longing to relax with a book it seems like the last straw, but what man doesn't expect his wife to take it in her stride? Buttons on shirts, darns to socks, patches to curtains, bed-linen, table-linen, kitchen cloths. They all take their share of time. And of course, there's always the personal sewing, making over and freshening up.

The routines she suggests are grouped under headings and described with a breezy cheerfulness ('bedmaking can be quite a pleasant interlude from the dusting and sweeping'), rather than arranged in strict time-table form; but in content they closely resemble the orders to servants issued in earlier domestic manuals and which were still listed as such in contemporary works such as the *Book of Good Housekeeping*, published by the magazine of which Kay Smallshaw had been editor.

For the publication of her book was in itself a reflection of a dramatic slowdown of women's march towards independence. Housewives had been heroines during the war, keeping the Home Front going as well as holding down jobs vital to the nation's wartime well-being, contriving culinary miracles despite rationing, remarkably glamorous in their shortened utility skirts and ARP warden uniforms. What had made them able to do so much for the war effort was the generous

****

provision made by industry for part-time work and job-sharing, British Restaurants in every high street, lunch canteens in factories and schools and the setting-up of nurseries for pre-school children.

But when the men came home, they wanted their jobs back, and their wives at home to nourish them and their children. Most women then thought that that was what they wanted too, visualising themselves, as Smallshaw puts it, 'in a dream house or flat; a charming hostess, clever housewife and adorable sweetheart all in one'. And of course a mother. 'Rearing babies through happy, healthy childhood to independent maturity is even more important than wiring aeroplanes, and is a very much more absorbing and exacting task' declared Gertrude Williams in her 1945 contribution to the New Democracy series, *Women and Work*.

Expectations of post-war domestic bliss were soon dashed. The postwar years were a time of austerity and rationing, contriving and making do. The middle-class was especially hard-hit. Labour's 'New Jerusalem' of a welfare state, a national health service, extended education and nationalised industries required much higher taxation: 9s in the pound (i.e. 45%) instead of the 4s 6d it had been before the war. Reduced incomes made fulltime domestic help unaffordable at a time when it was anyway hard to find. Servants had numbered over 1.5 million in 1901, but new opportunities in light industry and clerical work had arisen for the girls who had once applied for jobs as housemaids and cooks. The exodus of servants accelerated in the early years of the war, and by 1951 there were only some 750,000, falling to

200,000 in 1961. Most of these were moreover 'daily trotters-in' rather than resident maids, working far shorter hours, paid generously and jealously guarded from covetous female friends.

Committed to keeping up appearances, middle-class wives and mothers were soon run ragged. Mollie Panter-Downes' *One Fine Day* (1947) accurately maps the unsuccessful struggle of Laura and Stephen to keep up appearances. 'Wretched victims of their class, they still had dinner', and Stephen wistfully remembers the old days when 'Ethel or Violet, smart in their pretty uniforms' used to trip out into the garden to take away the coffee tray, 'bearing it away with a whisk of an apron streamer, a gleam of a neat ankle'; yet he knew it was 'preposterous how dependent he and his class had been on the anonymous caps and aprons who lived out of sight and worked the strings'. How people like Stephen and Laura actually fared we can deduce from later stories by the same author, collected as *Minnie's Room:* the peacetime stories of Mollie Panter-Downes (Persephone Books, 2002), that tell of maids giving their notice, emigration to the colonies and eccentric elderly couples unable to adjust to modern times.

Marghanita Laski's 1952 *The Village* (Persephone Books, 2004) is another perceptive commentary, mapping both the agonies undergone by women like Wendy Trevor, who 'loathed everything about housework' and was 'constantly resentful of the circumstances that against all her reasonable expectations had forced her to do it' and her daughter Margaret's longings to submerge herself in efficient little domesticities: 'every night before she went to sleep, Margaret saw herself as married, saw herself in a kitchen cooking, in a living-room knitting, in the streets with her ration-books, pushing a pram.' Significantly, the only way Margaret can achieve her dream is to marry the son of the charwoman her mother can no longer afford to employ, who has embarked on a promisingly prosperous career as a printer. Her parents' horror is so great that they beg the couple to emigrate to save their social face locally: the reconciliation between the classes so ardently hoped for by the new Labour government after the war was painfully slow in coming.

Things could have been otherwise. There had been a lively debate after the war as to the propriety of married women working. Beveridge respected housewives and acknowledged the arduousness of their lives, but thought women belonged in the home – not least because 'as mothers [they] have vital work to do in ensuring the adequate continuance of the British race and of British ideals in the world'. At the Labour Party conference of 1946, the Fabian Group claimed that housewives were becoming 'the oppressed proletariat of the modern world', and Ian Mikardo argued for 'communal central kitchens with a hot meals delivery service, properly staffed nurseries and central play rooms, district heating centres and even communal sewing centres'. Behind this generosity lay anxieties about population decline after the war. The Standing Joint Committee of Working Women's Organisations warned that housewives were beginning 'to buy a little independence with the tin-opener and birth control', and that 'if this has led to unfortunate results for the community, then the community must bear the blame for its neglect of the worker in the home'.

****

But the post-war economic crisis meant that nothing could be spared from the national coffers. Part-time work suddenly became impossible for industry to arrange, and the canteens and nurseries, which would do so much for working women in Scandinavia and France, were closed down.

Seen in this context, Smallshaw's assumption that middle-class women should now be their own servants was a capitulation, the sign of a battle lost. As a former editor of *Good Housekeeping*, and current editor of *Modern Woman*, she might have been expected to approach the business of running one's home without help from the point of view of a working wife, but she knew that in 1949 women like herself were in the minority. She does have a short chapter on 'Part-time Housewife', but the career woman she describes as only needing to give the house a 'brisk once-over before leaving for work' and 'paring down routines to the bone' is not married.

> With a married couple, unless sex differences are forgotten and the work is shared fifty-fifty, the strain on the wife may well be too great. A man about the house usually makes more work than he performs! When there are children, outside help is essential, unless days are to become ceaseless toil.

Men are conceded to have a degree of domestic usefulness in a later chapter, 'A Man About the House', but not, it seems, for much beyond bringing in the coal, seeing to the boiler, and washing up. In the infancy of the television age, children were apparently 'eager to help' from the age of five; both boys and

****

girls should be encouraged to pitch in and should be able to cook a simple meal and clear it away by the time they are in their teens. But 'it is, very rightly, Mother who does the lion's part and keeps the whole machine running sweetly'.

Again, Smallshaw reflects the changing nature of home life. One reason children added 'ceaseless toil' to the domestic scene was there were more of them; a widespread belief that it was selfish not to have a large family in the face of dire predictions of Britain's aging population brought a baby boom. At the same time, fashions had shifted from the rigid routines of Truby King and the controlling behaviourism of JB Watson to the attentive tenderness recommended by Dr Spock in his 1946 *Common Sense Book of Baby and Childcare*. Nor could much help be hoped for from older siblings after the introduction of the 1944 Education Act and the extension of both the school day and years spent in education. Margaret Trevor's sister Sheila in *The Village* turns up her nose at helping out at home; her driving ambition is to be 'Senior Mathematics mistress at whatever happened to be the best girl's school in England'.

What was urgently needed was a way of taking the drudgery out of housework so that the 'homemaking as a career' popularised by such experts as Margaret Bondfield and Eva Hubback could become more attractive. Since its first publication in 1922, *Good Housekeeping* had prided itself both on glamourising housekeeping and lessening the burden on 'the house-proud woman in these days of servant shortage' by bringing to her notice 'every new invention that is practical and economical in use'. 'The time spent on housework can

****

be enormously reduced in every home, without any loss to its comfort, and often with a great increase to its well-being and its air of personal care and attention' declared its first editorial. Thor washing machines (one with an unlikely attachment enabling it to peel potatoes), Goblin vacuum cleaners, Swan electric kettles, Rinso for whiter-than-new whites, Prosan preserving jars and Prestcold fridges were all praised for their contributions to lessening the load on the single-handed housewife – and made the trained, unionised and well-paid domestic staff dreamed of by Mrs Havelock Ellis in her *Democracy in the Home* less and less likely. Hottest news in 1949 was the opening of the first 'self-service laundry centre' by the Bendix company; appointments had to be booked and for 2s 6d a nine-pound bundle of laundry was washed, triple-rinsed and damp-dried; for a further penny another machine dried it to ironing stage. Smallshaw's experience on the magazine made her enthusiastic about both new inventions and time- and labour-saving arrangements. She suggests converting a typical small Victorian house by making the ground floor back room, usually used as a study, into a spacious kitchen next door to the front dining-room [the sitting room was evidently on the first floor], and its cramped back kitchen into either a day nursery or 'a masculine den'.

But the final effect of reading *How to Run your Home without Help* is profound relief that today clean air acts, central heating, easy-clean surfaces and wonderfully effective domestic appliances have made it much easier to skimp on housework. Clothes are now so cheap that few people bother with mending, and supermarkets and restaurants have transformed the

****

daily chore of cooking and food preparation into an optional hobby. From Smallshaw's pages we can glean the perfect way to make a cup of tea and useful tips on patching much loved garments, and be grateful that we no longer need to worry about how to blue the whites. Best of all, today we can hire professional cleaners to descend on our house and zip around them 'doing the rough' once a week.

However, just at present, I have decided not to. Smallshaw quotes a Dutch proverb: 'Any woman can clean a house; it takes a wise woman to keep it clean'. It is a challenge which has encouraged me to consider the possibility of doing my own housework, and, wonder of wonders, establishing that most despised of domestic habits, a cleaning routine. Like Dorothy Whipple's Ellen, I like looking after things. To my mind, traditional housework is just as enjoyable a hobby as making Game Pie or Sussex Pond Pudding, with the added advantage that it is much better for your figure. I like the process of polishing old brass and timeworn furniture; arranging posies in odd corners and baking orange skins in the Aga's slow oven to use as firelighters. The children have now all moved to homes of their own, and I have been reading Smallshaw's book just after moving to a rambling old-fashioned house which whispers to me that it would enjoy being cherished along old-fashioned lines. It is, after all, as freshly-painted, clean and tidy as it ever will be. The routine I envisage is delightfully simple: dust and hoover upstairs on Monday afternoons and downstairs on Tuesday afternoons, to be skipped on occasion if it doesn't suit me; self-indulgent polishing of furniture, silver and brass when I feel like it. I may not dust lampshades or wipe

****

the paintwork as often as Smallshaw advises, but I have bought nostalgically-scented Black Bison furniture polish and tile polish from Gills the Ironmonger, and blackleaded the grate; I might even experiment with holystoning the doorstep (if I can find any holystone) and trying out goose feathers on the tops of the books in the bookshelves. For in my heart of hearts I agree with Smallshaw rather than the feminists who rubbished housework so comprehensively in the 1970s. 'Running a home may seem unspectacular and ordinary, but making a success of it, so that the home is a happy one for all who live in it, is creative work to rank with the best. Exhausting though it may be, it enriches the personality.'

Christina Hardyment
Oxford, 2005

HOW TO RUN YOUR HOME WITHOUT HELP

INTRODUCTION

ALMOST every woman sees herself as a good home-maker. Before marriage she pictures herself in a dream house or flat; a charming hostess, clever housewife and adorable sweetheart all in one.

When she finds out that a lot of work has to go into serving those delicious little dinners, and that washing-up, dusting, cleaning and bed-making eat up her days, the vision is apt to get tarnished.

Yet it shouldn't. All work has its snags as well as its good points. There's nothing more monotonous about housework than there is in pounding a typewriter or modelling dresses or lots of other jobs that have a more glamorous reputation. Some of the tasks are dirty, some physically tiring. But given a little common savvy one can get less grubby working in the home than spending a day in a city office. As for fatigue, who wouldn't rather be bodily tired out than mentally exhausted?

The real difficulty facing the single-handed housewife is not knowing the 'how'. In the past, domestic work was poorly paid, so the false idea has grown up that anyone could do it without any special knowledge. Of course, the opposite is nearer the truth. Unless it's efficiently organised as well as carried out, it will take up too much time and effort. Especially now that labour is scarce, brains must have full play.

All work is coloured by the spectacles worn. Look on it as fearful drudgery and it will never be anything else. See it as a job supremely worth doing, some of it creative, some more humdrum, but all demanding one's best, then running the home without help becomes a challenge and rewarding in itself.

And what compensations it has! To be able to do things one's own way, even to the mistakes, and to have only one time-table to consider. To possess the kitchen absolutely at any time, and to have no other hand to mix up and sully all the precious tools! These freedoms alone are worth a lot.

But whether home-making without help is choice or necessity, the main thing is to do it as well, and as satisfyingly, as possible. To show the way to all those who must be both mistress and maid is the purpose of this book.

CONTENTS

CONTENTS

Chapter I

WHAT RUNNING A HOME ENTAILS

THERE used to be a pleasant myth that women staying at home to 'keep house' had a nice, sheltered, easy time. Sheltered perhaps, but even in the days of ample paid help, the woman who took any active part didn't find time hang on her hands. For the trouble—and, yes, the charm too—of domestic work is its infinite variety. No sooner is one job finished, than there's another sitting up and begging to be tackled.

Take cooking now. Even the most obdurate of the 'can't imagine why you want to do that' school of husbands will admit the necessity for preparing food. What isn't realised by those without the experience are the preliminaries that nowadays have to be put in. Shopping calls for concentrated paper work, allocating 'points' and thinking of alternatives, before any active steps are taken. As for the marketing itself, however done, it uses up a sizeable amount of time. Then there's the washing-up; no getting away from *that.* Even a cup of tea has to be cleared away. Regularly as morning comes, so do beds have to be remade. After use a bath needs cleaning, the lavatory basin gets dirty. Rooms attract dust with incredible speed and regularity. In many houses, and for most of the year, one fire at least has to be cleared out and relaid. Day in, day out, these routines have to be gone through.

Even so, these daily attentions only scratch the surface of the real house-cleaning that must be done if even a small flat or house is not to get a horrid, neglected look. The flick with the duster and the quick run over with the carpet sweeper answer only if something more thorough takes place once a week. Mirrors *will* go dull and streaky, and finger-marks appear on paintwork even without children about. And however careful you seem to be, floors in bathroom and kitchen become splodged with unsightly marks unless given regular attention.

In most small households there is not enough plate to worry about, but spoons and forks and the wedding-present silver do call for rubbing up with polish every so often. By the time gloves are donned and the brush used for the chased bits on the salver, it takes much longer than one ever thought. Glass and china in use isn't much trouble, but what a shock when the best tea service is taken from the back of the cupboard covered with a film of dust. Why is it that all cupboards seem to let in some dirt? Every one of them needs some periodic attention. So do light curtains and covers that cry out to be changed much too often. Of course, country dwellers don't suffer in this respect as much as those with compact little town flats. But town or country, tools need quite frequent inspection, ranging from the daily emptying of the carpet sweeper to the occasional shampooing given to the mop.

Then there's laundry. It's easy to say "Send it out", but what about stockings and lingerie, and those socks that shrink up at once if not treated tenderly? And supposing the service falls behind into the third week, by no means uncommon these days. Some washing, and ironing too, must be taken into consideration.

Few of us live in monastic seclusion, or want to. Half the fun of having a home is being able to invite people in. But entertaining, however simple, means another cake, or fresh trolley-cloths, or some more glasses to wash. Extra work again. The same with the finishing touches, the little things that add so much to the enjoyment of the home. Flowers make all the difference to a room, and can add anything from a few minutes to an hour on to the schedule. Altering the furniture round, experimenting with the pictures, rearranging the books or gramophone records—well, you can't call them work, but a whole evening can easily be whiled away in such pleasant pottering, while the mending basket remains untouched.

That mending! When you're longing to relax with a book it seems like the last straw, but what man doesn't expect his wife to take it in her stride? Buttons on shirts, darns to socks, patches to curtains, bed-linen, table-linen, kitchen cloths. They all take their share of time. And, of course, there's always personal sewing, making over and freshening up.

Does it seem an overwhelming list of duties? Let's face it, there's no eight-hour day about running a home. On the other hand, work *can* be fitted into a somewhat elastic time-table, and some of it, at least, would be done by most women for choice, whether they had any other 'full time' job or not.

So far, though, there's been no mention of any relaxation or leisure. Yet more, perhaps, than anyone else, the woman at home, alone all day with her multifarious tasks, needs some time for talk, for outside interests, and for plain fun. Without some such let-up, it's scarcely possible to be a complete success at home-making, however efficient the bare house-keeping.

At this stage you may wonder whether it can be done at all! The best answer is that thousands of women do achieve it and find it a good life. But for those of you who haven't had any previous experience, or who have never had to take in the rough as well as the smooth of running a house, here are two suggestions. First, rope in your husband to do a regular share. He won't be alone in giving a hand. And what a difference it makes if you can rely on the boiler being stoked, supper things washed and the weekend vegetables prepared. Secondly, and this depends on you alone, have a plan. The way to go about this is the substance of the next chapter.

Chapter II

HAVE A PLAN

"RISE at 6.45 a.m.; wash, dress and air bed. 7.5 a.m., clean out and re-lay sitting-room fire; tidy, sweep and dust room. 7.30 a.m., prepare breakfast. 7.45 a.m., serve breakfast. 8.15 a.m., clear away and wash up. 8.45 a.m., make beds. . . ." This was the sort of time-table given in the older books on household management. It assumes that everything is done with lightning speed, and no pause for let-up. Few can work with such clockwork precision, or want to.

On the other hand, it's equally fatal to start with the first job to hand and then go blithely on to the next, without having some rough guide as to how long can be allowed for each. This way you'll find the morning gone before you know where you are.

The generally accepted, and most satisfactory plan, is to divide the day's work into three main parts.

1. DAILY TIDYING UP AND QUICK CLEANING.

This includes bed-making, dusting, sweeping and putting straight the rooms, making the bathroom and lavatory presentable, and also the front porch, hall and stairs. It may take anything from an hour to two or more, according to the size of the home, the number of people in it, and the general tidiness of all concerned.

2. SHOPPING, FOOD PREPARATION AND CLEARING AWAY.

Breakfast, lunch, tea and dinner have to be planned, shopped for, cooked or otherwise produced, and then cleared away again. Three to four hours a day are a fair average to spend.

3. THE WEEKLY 'SPECIAL' WORK.

Monday it's washing day, Tuesday turning out the bedrooms, Wednesday the sitting-room gets the lion's share, and so on, right through the week. Every day, except perhaps the weekend, has its appointed task. You can ear-mark two to three hours a day for this.

CIRCUMSTANCES ALTER CASES.

Let's see how the day is going. 1–2½ hours for the daily tidying; 3–4 hours for shopping, cooking and washing-up, and 2–3 hours for house-cleaning, washing and other big jobs. That's good enough as a starting point, but exactly how the time is allotted between the three groups must depend upon individual cases.

What would be a perfect plan for Mrs. A, just married, with a sparsely furnished small flat, wouldn't work well for

Mrs. B. *Her* husband has just retired on a pension, and with their income reduced, she is doing without household help for the first time. Over the years she has accumulated precious possessions. Her crowded rooms, elegant with valued china and ornaments, will need far more time spent on them than the new bride's shining-new little home. On the other hand, the B's live very quietly, while the young A's love to entertain, which means a lot more cooking to be done.

Then there's the shopping question. Those who live near the shops can often whittle off a valuable half-hour from this task. To balance this, a country district may have such a good service of tradesmen calling that personal visits to the shops are scarcely necessary.

Which is more valuable, money or time? If budgeting has to be very close, it means more washing to be done at home. Mending and making over will demand more time. Windows may have to be cleaned. Cooking will be more strenuous if nothing may be bought that can be home-made. So the working day is lengthened.

In another household, it may be better planning to increase expenditure in some respects in order to save time, or energy. If health is not too good, more money spent on laundry or dry-cleaning, or a once-weekly visit from a 'char' (giving in return more leisure), may pay. Or buying canned soups or shop cake, instead of making them, can leave time for dress-making, or gardening.

Of course, where there are children, a good slice of the day must be devoted to them, so that means a different plan. As, however, this book is mainly for the newcomer to running a home, let's leave children out of the picture for the moment. Later on, in Chapter XVII, we'll consider the alterations in the household routine necessitated by the advent of a baby.

But to get back to our plan, or rather *yours*, for you must work out a rough time-table. When deciding on the schedule you'll follow, don't forget that, so far, time has been allowed for only the 'bare bones' of home-making. All the 'social graces' side, from the arranging of flowers to entertaining, is extra. So are the unconsidered trifles, such as checking the laundry, answering the door or phone or sudsing through precious nylons. Then there's mending and sewing of all kinds, and ironing, which must often be done out of routine working hours.

So because of these other necessary, but more personal jobs, not to mention relaxing and having a little pleasure, it's unwise to spend longer than the plan allows on the hard-core work. If you do, you'll get behindhand and over-done. Also you will run the risk of that occupational disease of housewives, which has taken the sweetness out of so many marriages; letting the house own you, instead of the other way about.

Chapter III

THE TOOLS FOR THE JOB

ONCE upon a time, the newly-married housewife used to complain of long, empty hours. Nowadays, "Time simply flies" is much more likely to be her theme song, at least if she has no help. To 'get round' at all she must have the best tools, and get the most out of them, too.

'Tools' is here used in the sense of all equipment necessary to the running of the house. Some of the most important tools are part of the fixtures, more's the pity, since they are the most difficult to alter, and often are full of faults.

Consider the sink. One can scarcely do a household job without spending some time at it. Yet how often is it too low, or placed in a bad light, or furnished with only one draining-board, and no space for another? Then there's the question of hot water. *Constant* hot water on tap does more to take the drudgery out of housework than anything else. Yet many a landlord thinks he's discharged his duty if the 'amenities' of the house or flat include a wasteful, temperamental boiler or an old-fashioned water-heater of uncertain performance.

HOT WATER PAYS.

If by any means at all it is possible to have an efficient hot-water system installed, do it. No amount of other labour-saving equipment will compensate for the frustration, lost time and sheer drudgery caused by an insufficient or erratic hot-water supply. Various types of water-heaters, for solid fuel, gas and electricity, are listed and briefly explained in Appendix I, pp. 174–181. Some of them involve capital expenditure only worthwhile for house owners. Into this class come the domestic boilers of different kinds, some supplying radiators as well. If the plumbing is already fixed, it may be less expensive than you think to have a new, labour-saving model substituted for the old, dirty, wasteful one. Or you may be able to make a conversion from, say, solid fuel to gas firing, that will pay in your case.

Supposing you live in a flat, or a rented house? There are small water-heaters that can be fixed over the kitchen sink or in the bathroom. These are comparatively inexpensive, and are also easily dismantled and taken away when you move. In fact, there's a solution for every hot-water problem, if you look for it.

THE SINK AND THE COOKER.

In the past, the sink itself was invariably a built-in fixture. New types of kitchen units, which include sink, draining-boards and various cupboards, all in one piece, can now be purchased in any good furnishing ironmongery department. For those converting an old house, or building a new one, these units offer many advantages. The ordinary tenant generally feels that taking out the landlord's sink and replacing it by one of his own would be too great an expense and undertaking. Measured in terms of saved work and effort, however, the cost might prove well worthwhile. This is especially so if the house is rented on a long lease. Examples of the types of sink fixture now on the market are given in Appendix I, page 198.

Some people would say that even the sink is less important than the cooker. Luckily these no longer 'come with the house', except in the case of built-in solid-fuel stoves. Even the latter can usually be replaced with a 'free-standing' type that can move with the tenant, just as a gas or electric cooker does.

So do get a good cooker, even if it means cutting down elsewhere. The post-war stoves, for gas, electricity and solid fuel, have big advantages over the average pre-war ones. They're lighter on fuel, easier to clean and much more fool-proof, something which even an experienced cook finds useful at times! Turn to Appendix I, pp. 186–190, for a few examples of representative models of various kinds.

WHAT KIND OF FIREPLACE?

Asked which is the dirtiest and most disliked household job, most women would say "Fires", meaning the daily cleaning out and re-laying of the sitting-room grate. Yet, though central heating, gas and electricity have their very good points for room heating, there's no doubt that an open fire, in one room of the house, at least, has a lot in its favour.

If you do have an open fireplace which you intend to use, have a good look at it before making out lists of labour-savers you'd like. Putting in a fresh grate that will make less dust and dirt and give more heat for less fuel would probably be a sound investment.

Don't think that a new grate must be a permanent 'landlord's fixture'. The new 'free-standing' kinds take very little fixing. If you move, they can go with you. Some have a kind of hood that will transform an open into a closed fire in a matter of seconds. Overnight, for instance, the hood is placed in position and the fire then keeps in all night, burning at a very slow rate. What a joy to come down to a warm room in the morning, finding only a little ash to empty, instead of the old misery of cleaning out cinders and flying dust!

Other grates heat by convection as well as radiation. This means that warmth comes into the room instead of escaping up the chimney. This extra heat can be carried up into a bedroom, by means of an air duct, if preferred. Then there are the new gas-coke grates. Instead of laying with wood and paper you simply pour in the coke and turn on the gas for ten minutes or so. The coke gives out a splendid heat and is much cleaner than soft coal. However, one of the advantages of most modern grates is that they will burn various kinds of fuel—a big point these days.

When there is no fixed gas-ignition, the gas or electric poker is a handy tool which costs very little, but saves a lot of time and work.

Some grates need fairly elaborate builder's work, and cost a good deal. Others again will pay for themselves in a year. Details of some representative kinds are given in Appendix I, pp. 181–183, but it does pay to get expert advice before choosing, as much depends upon the size of room, the way chimneys are built, and other points.

But supposing you favour gas or electricity for your fires? Well, still decide on the kind you'll have at an early stage in your home-equipment choosing. You see, there have been so many improvements in recent years that making do with serviceable-looking but wasteful old models will prove rather a poor economy. Much the same thing applies to those with their own homes who either have central heating already installed, or are toying with the idea. Appendix I, pp. 183–186, gives an idea of what is on the market; but, once again, go into the matter thoroughly.

HOW TO CHOOSE TOOLS.

Yes, choosing tools is more complex than it seems. From the most expensive piece of equipment to the cleaner used for the bath, care, thought and experience too are needed.

It's worth taking trouble, for your right choice will often make all the difference between being on top of the job and just scrambling through!

Two guides to follow are: first, don't rush into buying before you have seen what else is obtainable; secondly, as already mentioned, do take some expert advice. The latter is not hard to obtain. Appendix I in this book gives a guide to the kind of equipment now available. But new designs are always coming out and improvements being made. There are organisations whose business it is to keep right up to date on these matters.

On almost everything connected with the home the Council of Industrial Design can usually give a helpful lead, through the various excellent booklets it publishes; for instance, *How to Buy Things for the Kitchen, How to Buy Furniture,* etc. These can be bought from H.M. Stationery Office, Kingsway, London, W.C.2, and are very inexpensive. Then the various trade organisations, such as the Coal Utilisation Joint Council, The Women's Advisory Committee on Solid Fuel, the Electrical Development Association, the Electrical Association for Women, the British Gas Federation, and the Women's Gas Council, will be valuable in their own sphere. Turn to p. 201 in Appendix I for the respective addresses.

Other useful sources of information are the women's magazines. Their advice is knowledgeable, and usually very sound.

Remember that you need information of two kinds. The technical performance and running costs are important, but perhaps what matters even more is whether the particular tool will be likely to pay its way in *your* case. A good sink, with plentiful hot water, and efficient arrangements for heating and cooking are needed in every house. With much other equipment, individual circumstances must be weighed up.

In a country house with large tiled-floor kitchen, for example, a self-wringing mop, for daily swilling over, is almost a necessity. In a town flat, with linoleum or composition-covered floors in kitchen and bathroom, it would never be used. When rooms have polished floors, bare save for an occasional rug, an electrical floor polisher would be a good 'buy'. In the reverse case, when most of the floors are carpeted, a vacuum cleaner soon repays its cost, while the little bit of floor polishing can be done as quickly by hand.

But whatever the individual problems, every housewife has cleaning, cooking—which means preparation and food storage too—as well as laundry work and the inescapable washing-up to consider. For each class of work, the right tools do make all the difference. The following lists are given only as a very approximate guide, but they will serve as a starting point. You may dismiss some items as unnecessary; and of course budgets, numbers in family and personal preference must be considered. By and large, though, economise anywhere but on your tools. In Chapter XII, Method in the Kitchen, we'll go, in further detail, into the subject of cooking equipment, with what to look for and avoid. Any brides about to make out their shopping or wedding-present lists are advised to turn to pp. 102–103 first of all. Now for the general lists.

1. HOUSE-CLEANING TOOLS.

(*a*) Brooms, Brushes and Floor Mops.

Long-handled hair broom, stiff carpet brush, soft brush, long-handled cornice brush, upholstery whisk, blacklead brushes*, silver brush; dusting mop, self-wringing mop*, long-handled scrubber*, scrubbing brush. (The items marked with asterisks will not be required in some households at all.)

(*b*) Mechanical Cleaners.

Carpet sweeper, vacuum cleaner, floor polisher (hand or electric), hand suction cleaner.

(*c*) Dusters, Cloths, etc.

Dusters, plain and impregnated with furniture oil if liked; floor-cloths; separate cloths for each of the following: bath, lavatory, paintwork, also for applying metal and silver polish, floor-polish, furniture-cream, cleaner for mirrors; clean cloths for 'rubbing up'; two chamois leathers, one for dry silver polishing, one for 'damp leathering'; linen scrim for windows; dust-sheets.

(*d*) Cleaning Materials, etc.

Scouring powder (Vim, Mirro, or similar), soda, ammonia (powdered or liquid), liquid or cake soap substitute, or both kinds, bleaching liquid (Parozone, or similar); appropriate polishes for floors (wax), furniture, brass and copper, silver, mirrors (Windolene, or similar); powdered whitening, methylated spirits, turps substitute, oxalic acid (when obtainable); liquid and powder disinfectant; fine and medium steel wool; dry-cleaning grease solvent (Thawpit, or similar).

(*e*) Miscellaneous.

Dustpan and pail.

2. COOKING TOOLS.

(*a*) Saucepans, etc., for Use on the Stove or in the Oven.

Saucepans in various sizes with lids; steamer; double-saucepan; frying-pans; casseroles of metal, fireproof china or glass; baking tins, cake tins, tart and bun tins; pudding dishes and basins; kettle.

(*b*) For Food Preparations.

Mixing bowl, pastry-board and rolling-pin, flour-dredger, pastry-cutter, pastry brush; chopping-board; egg-whisk, mincer, graters; colander, strainers, sieve; lemon-squeezer; vegetable brush; measuring spoons and jug; scales.

(*c*) Kitchen Cutlery.

Ladle, perforated ladle; fish-slice; cooking-tongs; potato-peeler; kitchen scissors; short-bladed vegetable-knife, one or more cook's knives for filleting, chopping, etc., palette-knife, utility knife; wooden spoon, two or three metal spoons in different sizes; two or three forks; can-opener, bottle-opener, corkscrew.

OPTIONAL EXTRAS FOR COOKING. Pressure cooker or pressure saucepan; preserving-pan, thermometer, steriliser; electric mixer; juice-extractor; potato-ricer; butter-shaper.

(*d*) For Food Storage.

Cool larder, preferably with a meat safe; refrigerator; dry-goods cupboards or shelves; vegetable rack or drawer.

(*e*) For Washing-up.

Basin, sink-tidy, mop, bottle-mop, tea-pot-spout cleaner, saucepan brush, dish-cloth, tea-towels; steel wool and water softener of some kind.

(*f*) Miscellaneous.

Waste bin.

3. LAUNDRY WORK TOOLS.

Bowls or small bath; washing machine or wash-boiler (independent or small one to go on top of stove); wringer; clothes-lines and pegs; drying cabinet or clothes airer; ironing-board with sleeve attachment or board, ironing-pad and cloth; electric or gas iron; soapflakes, soap powder, washing soap, liquid and powder soap substitute, laundry blue, starch, bleach and borax.

So much for the tools. How to use them to best advantage we'll discuss in subsequent chapters dealing in more detail with the various categories of work. In the next chapter, let's take a look at another aspect of labour-saving, the arrangement of the home.

Chapter IV

LAYOUT OF THE HOME

"It's so hard on the feet," was the reply of a new housewife when asked how she liked 'being at home'. She'd been used to sedentary work in an office. Now she found that when she wasn't standing she was trotting to and fro. While working, she never seemed to sit down at all.

With a little thought and practice, some standing jobs, such as preparing vegetables and ironing, can be done sitting down. All the same, one covers a lot of ground looking after even a small house.

That is why it is so important to arrange rooms to obviate unnecessary journeys. The dining-room, now. Is it next door to the kitchen, so that food can be served with the minimum of exertion and the maximum of speed? Or does it mean several journeys, at least, down a long corridor before and after every meal? Even worse, is there a flight of stairs to be negotiated?

This sort of thing is bad enough when the work of running

a house is shared. When everything falls on one pair of shoulders, it becomes uncommonly like drudgery.

Possible remedies are three. To move either dining-room or kitchen, or to combine them.

STUDY INTO KITCHEN.

In a small Victorian terrace house at Chelsea, the study was ruthlessly commandeered and transformed into a kitchen. It lay immediately behind the little ground-floor dining-room, while the original kitchen was down a couple of steps and along a narrow passage at the back. There had been folding doors, since sealed up, between the dining-room and the study. It was now a small matter to have a single door and a service hatch placed in the partitioning to make the rooms intercommunicating again.

The new kitchen has the advantage of an east aspect, and as the window looks on to a narrow slit of the garden shaded by the wall of the old kitchen, the room does not get too hot for working comfort. The old kitchen had the window on the south side, the worst possible position.

Gas and electric points were already installed, but a certain amount of plumbing work had to be done to bring the water supply from the original kitchen. All the old kitchen fitments were obsolete and work-making, so these were not moved into the new quarters. Instead, factory-made units, all of uniform depth, were chosen.

Although appreciably smaller, the new kitchen seems more roomy, as the compact fixtures hold more than the old open dresser and low cupboards. Laundry equipment, including an automatic washing machine, has been installed, so that now almost all the wash is done at home. In the old days, the antiquated copper in the scullery was never used, and it was drudgery trying to wash clothes in the low, shallow kitchen sink.

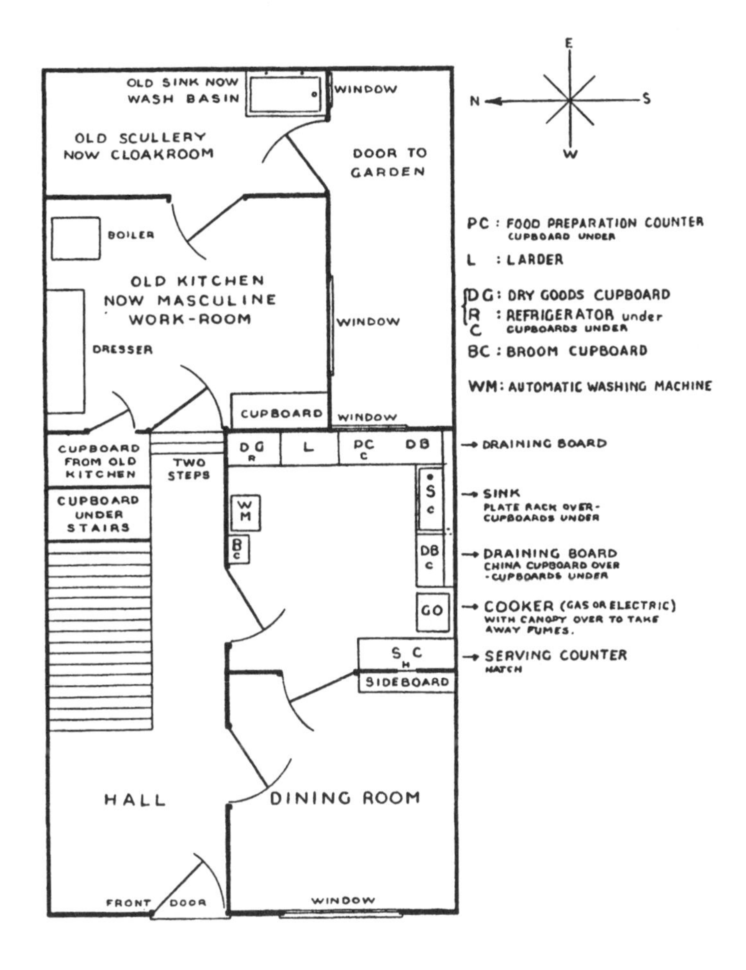

VICTORIAN TERRACE HOUSE. OLD STUDY, BEHIND DINING ROOM, TRANSFORMED INTO MODERN KITCHEN.

The conversion has meant a certain amount of capital outlay, but to balance this the mistress of the house finds she can manage as easily single-handed now as she did with regular help before. And, of course, the value of the property has been improved.

KITCHEN INTO MASCULINE 'DEN'.

The old kitchen hasn't been left derelict. It has become a workshop for the master of the house, and is vastly more to his taste than his old study. The fact that the floor is tiled is an advantage rather than otherwise, especially now that the room is no longer damp. An efficient streamlined boiler, needing once-a-day fuelling only, has been substituted for the old temperamental model. This provides all the domestic hot water in winter. Also it keeps the workshop warm and heats the small radiators that have been installed in the first-floor drawing-room and the bedrooms. In summer, an immersion-heater in the tank saves lighting the boiler.

Although they were obsolete in a kitchen, the old dresser and cupboards fit nicely into the workshop scheme. The dresser looks quite decorative set off with polished pewter pots and similar trophies. The cupboards take tools, stores, paint, wood and all the impedimenta of the amateur handyman. Even the scullery beyond has a new rôle. As an extra cloakroom for men visitors and their host, it has provided a valuable addition to the house's amenities.

A DOWNSTAIRS DAY NURSERY.

In this particular household the only child is a schoolboy son, who enjoys the workshop as much as his father. If there had been small children, however, the room could have been converted into an excellent day nursery. With its exit through the old scullery into the tiny garden, and its proximity to the new kitchen, the placing couldn't have been better.

Sometimes, when the kitchen is in the basement and the dining-room on the ground floor, a similar conversion to the above is practicable. When, however, there is no room, not even a large cloakroom, that can be made into a respectable kitchen, it's better to eat downstairs.

Some years ago, when the fashion was for very tiny kitchens, the usual conversion was to transform the scullery, that usually went with the Victorian or Edwardian kitchen, into a working kitchen, and the kitchen proper into a dining-room. This rarely left room for laundry space. Also it tended to discourage a helping hand from husband or children, as there simply wasn't room for more than one person to turn round at once.

SCULLERY INTO DINING NICHE . . .

An alternative worth considering is to make the scullery, which usually leads into the garden, into a dining niche, and have a more generous-sized kitchen proper. This involves moving the sink, but as a new one would probably have been necessary anyway, the extra trouble is slight.

. . . OR INTO UTILITY ROOM.

If the kitchen is big enough to include dining space, the scullery converts readily into a 'utility' room for laundry work, doing the flowers, shoe cleaning and similar jobs best done away from the food preparation. Two new sinks, one in the kitchen, one in the utility room, are then required.

Such drastic transformations as these are not always possible. There is the question of cost, and that of getting a licence. Besides, as often as not, there is no spare room which can have its use altered. This is usually the case if you live in a flat. The problem here is either to find room for taking meals in the kitchen in circumstances that are not too crowded or disagreeable, or to minimise the difficulties of carrying food and utensils an appreciable distance.

MEALS IN THE KITCHEN.

If, as is often the case in a flat, you can't have a special fixed dining corner in the kitchen, there are three possible arrangements. In a biggish room, a centre table or a permanent table under a window are both good. Where space is tight, make it a folding table similarly placed, or a flap table or counter against a wall. For a family of two the latter is quite a possible solution.

Whichever you choose, do have the furniture as nice as possible. A table and chairs that are pleasing to the eye won't cost a great deal more than old junk, but how they will 'dress up' the room! It's the same with napery and china. Have it simple and suitable by all means, but if eating in the kitchen is to be the rule, see that meals get the sauce of attractive service and pleasant surroundings.

WHEN DINING-ROOM AND KITCHEN ARE TOO FAR APART.

If, on the other hand, you must eat in a room some distance from where the food is prepared, do have a good roomy trolley. Preferably get one with drawers, in which the amount of cutlery normally used for a meal can be kept. Otherwise, keep a small plate-box or basket on the lower shelf. It's a good plan to cover one shelf with easy-to-clean, heat-resisting mats. Saucepans or casseroles can then, if necessary, be loaded straight on to it. If matched aluminium pans, of the kind that can be used in the oven or on the hot-plate, are used, they can be taken right into the dining-room without looking amiss.

In the dining-room, try to have a hot-plate or plate-warmer. Electric, and occasionally gas, types are obtainable, as well as the old spirit-lamp ones for those who live without main services. These table hot-plates are good-looking but rather expensive, unless you can get one second-hand, but they do remove the risk of having food spoiled through being half cold. (*See* Appendix I, p. 200.)

Though the kitchen is usually the more convenient place for storing china in daily use, providing the space is available, keep cruet, sugar sifter and any extras likely to be wanted on the table, right at hand in the dining-room. At the same time, get in the habit of mentally checking them over after each meal when the table is cleared. You can then load on to the trolley anything that needs refilling or other attention.

If coffee is taken at table after a meal, an electric percolator, or similar machine that can be plugged in on the spot, is worthwhile. So is an electric kettle and a toaster, if toast is liked. In fact, any cooking that can be done at the table, such as making waffles for the sweet course, will certainly simplify proceedings. (*See* Appendix I, pp. 199–200, for equipment details.)

Careful meal-planning will help too, so that all courses can be brought into the dining-room at the beginning of a meal. Some suggestions for this kind of labour-saving are given in Chapter XIX, on Entertaining.

USING ROOMS TO BEST ADVANTAGE.

There is one aspect of layout of the home that hasn't been considered so far. It's that of using the space to best suit one's way of living, and not necessarily to a formal pattern.

Supposing, in a family of four, two of which are young children, the accommodation is the popular 'two reception downstairs and three bedrooms up'. The conventional way is to use one 'recep' as a dining-room, and one bedroom as a nursery. But how can a single-handed mother cope with a children's day room upstairs? She can't literally be in two places at once. Better to transform the dining-room into a day nursery and abandon any idea of a separate room for meals while the children are small. The parents' dinner or supper can be taken on a folding table in the sitting-room. For the day-time family meals, the kitchen or the nursery must be used.

Upstairs, the second largest of the bedrooms will be the children's night nursery. The third can become a 'den' for the man of the house, or a guest-room-cum-study with a desk for letter-writing, tackling accounts, or other tasks that demand quiet.

When there are no children, planning becomes easier. It's surprising, though, how many women give themselves unnecessary work because they use their home in the way the house agent described the rooms, rather than to suit their own convenience. Also, they get less value from it than they might, simply because they allow themselves to get in a rut and don't change the rooms around enough to suit their current way of living. Look on your home as a background to be moulded as far as possible to your needs, and not a frame which you must endeavour to fill according to a prearranged pattern!

Chapter V

PLANNING THE KITCHEN

"I CAN always tell the experienced housewife," said the estate agent. "She goes straight to the kitchen, looks at the sink and the larder, and then goes into a sort of trance. She's weighing it up to see how everything will fit in, and so forth." He was right. To the woman at home, the kitchen is all-important. It's the workshop where most of her day is spent. In the past women have patiently put up with all kinds of inconveniences in kitchens designed by men, who gave no thought to the problems concerned. To do that to-day, when help is out of the picture and life so much more exacting, is real folly.

We can't all have the streamlined masterpieces that meet our admiring gaze in the show-houses at exhibitions, but a kitchen that's labour-saving and pleasant is not so hard to achieve.

The essentials are: (1) adequate working surface; (2) sufficient storage accommodation, including a well-ventilated cool larder or a refrigerator; (3) good light, air and enough sun or gaiety in decoration to give a lift to the spirits; (4) easily-washable steam-resisting walls, and a floor easy to keep clean; (5) adequate ventilation; and (6), as discussed in Chapters III and XII, good tools.

GOOD ARRANGEMENT IS ALL IMPORTANT.

Many kitchens with all these features still fall short of the mark because the arrangement is bad. The china cupboard is at the other end of the room from the sink. The larder and the rest of the food storage are at opposite corners, and both quite a way from the stove. Every job takes twice the time it needs, and uses up twice as much energy, too.

Cooking is the kitchen's main function, so that if everything needed in the storage, preparation and clearing away of food is in the most logical, natural order, steps will be saved, working simplified.

But unless there's a separate utility room, which is still the exception rather than the rule, other jobs have to be done in the kitchen, too. Chief of these is clothes washing. Ideally, the washing machine or wash-boiler should be built in next to the sink, so that clothes can be 'wrung' from one to the other. Unless it is a completely self-contained automatic model, the machine should be placed where it can easily be moved into position next to the sink.

Yes, there is a lot to consider in deciding on the layout. Kitchen planning experts say there are three sound ways of grouping the fixtures, according to the size, shape, lighting and aspect of a room. In a narrow corridor kitchen, compactness is essential, so the working equipment is placed all down one side. The other two alternatives, suitable for bigger, oblong or square rooms, are the corner, and bay or three-sided placings. In all, the aim is to preserve, as far as possible, the correct working sequence for cooking (which means food storage, counters for food preparation, cooker, sink, then

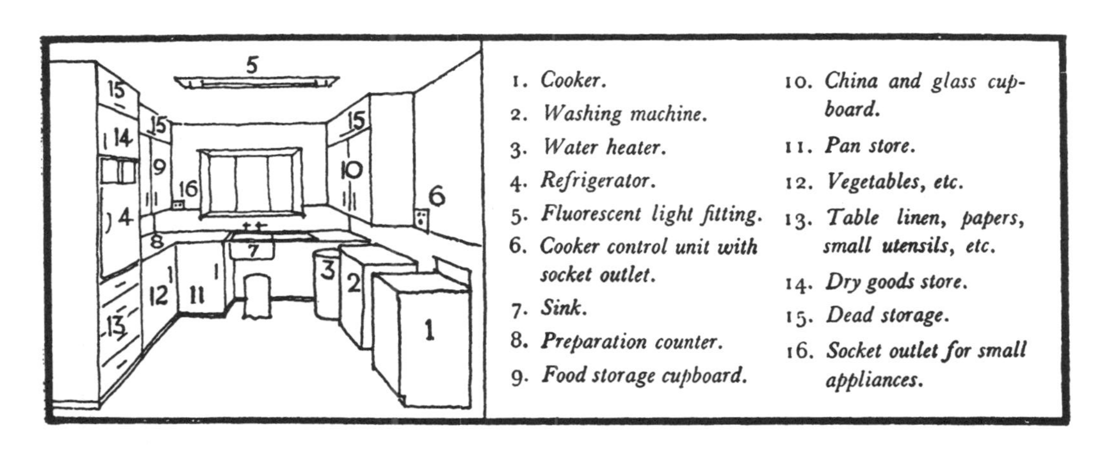

ELECTRIC KITCHEN, DESIGNED FOR THE SMALL CONTEMPORARY HOUSE BY THE ELECTRICAL DEVELOPMENT ASSOCIATION.

china and utensil storage), while getting a good light and having the rest of the equipment conveniently to hand.

A good example of kitchen design for the small contemporary house is the electric kitchen illustrated on p. 37. Six possible layouts for the typical one-hundred-square-feet-floor-area kitchen of a three-bedroomed, semi-detached house were mulled over by the technical staff of the Electrical Development Association. Each had some disadvantages to balance the other good features. In the version finally chosen, the correct working sequence is broken, but the advantages outweighed it. In a bay arrangement of this kind, no equipment is too far away to add materially to the work. The broom cupboard and drying cabinet, which are placed at the other end of the room, have not the same connection with actual kitchen work as the rest of the fixtures. This electric kitchen is planned as a workshop only, for a door leads into a small adjacent dining-room.

CONSIDER COMFORT, TOO.

Lighting.

If you look at the diagram you will see that the kitchen is well-lit both by the window and by the fluorescent ceiling strip. Lighting is very important. Often an additional bulb over the cooker, say, will add greatly to efficiency and comfort.

Height of Working Surfaces.

The need for comfort is often overlooked. A good deal of backache is caused by a too-low sink, not by the actual washing-up or clothes washing done in it. The same applies to many a kitchen table or other working surface. Standard-unit fixtures, used in the better modern kitchens, are usually 32 in. high, which is right for the average woman. The sensible thing to do is to experiment to find out the height most comfortable in your own case. Improvements can often be made quite simply.

A block of wood underneath the washing-up bowl and a stool of the right height will work wonders in cutting down fatigue.

VENTILATION.

One of the essentials mentioned earlier was ventilation. Walls running with condensed steam, and a clinging cooking smell, can make the best-arranged kitchen a far from pleasant place. Flinging open the window is the usual remedy, but in cold weather at least the cure can be worse than the complaint. A ventilated trunking over the cooker, coke boiler if any, and if possible over the sink, too, is the ideal. The trunking, which looks like a square canopy, has an outlet into a flue. It sucks up the steam without letting it escape into the room, and with it, of course, the smells. Alternatives, where there is no flue, are an extraction fan that can be fitted into the glass of the window, or a portable air purifier. Some details of such appliances are given in Appendix I, p. 197. Even a straightforward electric fan, fitted to an outside wall, will prove helpful.

WALLS.

Although steamy-looking walls are unpleasant, those that absorb the moisture are infinitely worse. Neither distemper nor a varnished wallpaper is suitable for a kitchen, and represent false economy. Half-tiled walls, with washable paint on upper half and ceiling, are probably the best choice, though glossy paint all over wears well and can be easily washed down. Don't be misled if you are told the distemper is washable. It is sometimes possible to sponge distemper in a room that gets ordinary wear, but the kitchen steam soon flakes off the surface and gives a sorry appearance.

FLOORS.

As far as the floor is concerned, don't put appearance first. The visitor to a tiled-floor kitchen may admire its freshness and hygienic look, but the woman who works there knows that the tiles are chilly to the feet and take too long to polish. A tiled-floor section where the cooking stove and independent boiler stand is sound sense. Otherwise good linoleum makes the most generally satisfactory floor covering, though compositions of the pitch-mastic kind are liked by some.

And talking of the hygienic look, this can be greatly overdone. A kitchen so tiled and white and shining that it resembles a hospital theatre is not the happiest background for a large part of the day. An attractive view from the window is perhaps the best picture of all. Otherwise, or as well if space permits, what about a gay print or poster, or some flowering plants on the window sill? In any case, a cheerful colour scheme helps. If meals are taken in the kitchen, do be realistic and use some of your furnishing money on it, rather than only on the bedrooms or lounge, which don't get nearly as much use.

INTELLIGENT SPENDING PAYS.

In fact, intelligent spending on the kitchen probably brings bigger returns in satisfaction than equivalent outlay on any other part of the house. Good-quality saucepans, for instance, as we'll stress in Chapter XII, Method in the Kitchen, do simplify cooking. But it isn't always a question of spending money. Using one's wits and improvisation often bring just as good results.

The Larder.

There's the larder, for example. Unless you are lucky enough to have a refrigerator as well, the aspect should be north or east, but this alone is not enough. If the window is more than a slit, a sun blind is necessary. This can be rigged up out of a length of canvas, a piece of broomstick, blind cord and a pulley wheel. Walls must be washable, if they're not to get greasy and grubby, but it's not a hard job to give them a couple of coats of washable paint. Shelves should be painted too, and one at least needs to be cool-surfaced. If no marble slab or tiled shelf has been fitted, try to get a piece of marble, say from an old washstand, cut to shape. Even easier, is to buy separate tiles, and place them close together to cover the shelf. Or use enamel meat-trays; they are cool and easily washable. Ideally, have a flyproof meat-safe and a ventilated vegetable rack inside the larder. If not, make liberal use of washable cheese-cloth to cover all perishables.

If you feel that your kitchen leaves very much to be desired, but you just can't launch out as you'd like; take heart. Most of us are in that boat. Even so, it's surprising what improvements can be made, even when the main equipment is fixed. Once you know the approved layout, you have a guide to follow when you begin to experiment. Otherwise, there is only the trial-and-error method, which can be surprisingly unreliable, judging by the work some people will go on giving themselves.

Just to give an idea of what can be done, without extravagant outlay, here is the story of three difficult kitchens, and how they have been improved.

AWKWARD KITCHEN (1).

In a semi-detached house built between the wars. As Plan A shows, the kitchen is small, oblong-shaped, and with two doors in a line. The larder is in the hall, outside the kitchen door. The closed-in dresser, which had to hold baking tins and casseroles as well as the china, is at the opposite end from the sink. There is very little food preparation space. All in all, the layout could scarcely be worse. To get the correct working sequence would be impossible without gutting the entire kitchen. Instead, the aim has been to cut down steps and simplify working.

Having to keep all foodstuffs in the larder was the first snag. To obviate that, a shallow fixture with shelves has been

PASSAGE BETWEEN
HOUSES

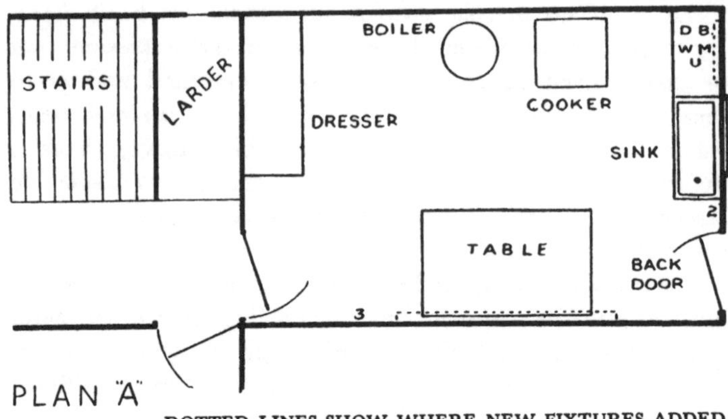

DOTTED LINES SHOW WHERE NEW FIXTURES ADDED

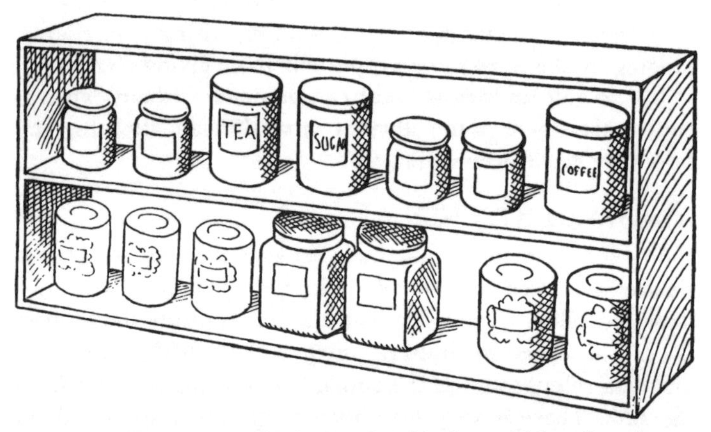

fixed to the long wall above the kitchen table. *See* above. The shelves are only four inches deep, which means they don't protrude too much and take only one row of tins or jars. This means that everything can be seen at a glance and easily handled. The fixture, part of an eight-foot one, originally built for a chemist's shop, was picked up at a sale.

It was then in a very grubby state. Now, cleaned and enamelled to match the kitchen walls, it's quite decorative, especially as the stores are kept in gaily-painted containers.

At the sink end of the fixture go tea, coffee, cocoa, sugar, salt, condiments for cooking and porridge oats. These are in most constant use, so are nearest to hand. Cereals, cornflour, custard powder, flour for sauce-making, gravy powder, bottled sauce and flavourings are arranged on the rest of the shelf space. All these are used in cooking, but perhaps not every day. This fixture cuts out some of the steps.

Next problem was to bring the china-storage and washing-up departments a little closer. In place of the old saucepan shelf, the roomiest possible plate-rack has been placed over the draining-board. This takes all plates in daily use. A cupboard, made by enclosing the space under the sink, accommodates baking tins and casseroles and some saucepans.

It would have been useful to have had another cupboard under the draining-board, but the space is needed for the wash-boiler. A further improvement hoped for one day is a new counter unit, with toe space and cupboards beneath, in place of the table. This would give the room needed for mixing-bowl and pastry-making implements, cake tins and pudding basins, now packed too tightly in the bottom of the cupboard dresser.

This kitchen has no broom cupboard. The cupboard under the stairs has been utilised for the purpose, by means of careful fitments.

AWKWARD KITCHEN (2).

In a flat in an old converted house. This kitchen is pleasantly roomy and bright. It is used for breakfast and midday lunch with the children. Plan C shows the general layout. One door, a good-sized window. An old-fashioned, unused kitchener takes up the centre of a third wall; the big open dresser most of the fourth.

Principal drawback is the scattered placing of equipment. Having the gas cooker next to the larder is unsatisfactory, too. All the china, casseroles and baking tools were kept in the dresser at the opposite end from the sink. The housemaid's box, cleaning materials and also the wringer took up the lower half of the built-in cupboard next to the kitchener with dry goods at the top. Soapflakes, water softener and other washing-up and washing necessaries found a place on a shelf over the sink. Brooms, ironing-board and sweeper had to lean against the wall next the sink, in default of a cupboard for them.

PLAN C

Plan D shows what can be done by regrouping. The gas stove and gas refrigerator have changed places. The old kitchener has been taken out and a cupboard for dry goods placed in the recess. Now all the food storage is together. Between the gas stove and the draining-board a cupboard unit with working-surface top has been installed. Saucepans, casseroles, baking tins and pastry-making equipment go in this cupboard. With a plate rack over the sink only the decorative china has to be put away on the open shelves of the dresser, so much traffic across the kitchen is saved. The lower half of the dresser makes a splendid place for bottled fruit, preserving-pan and other seldom-used articles.

PLAN D

A small washing machine, with porcelain table top and folding wringer, replaces the small table next the sink. Next to it a small cupboard taking the soap, water softener, etc., previously on the shelf, also provides a useful counter top. Finally, the old dry-goods cupboard next to the old kitchener has had half the shelving taken out so that the ironing-board, brooms, sweepers, etc., can be accommodated. There's room for the housemaid's box and cleaning materials in the remaining half.

The kitchen looks just as gay, but much more business-like, and work is certainly less tiring.

AWKWARD KITCHEN (3).

In a converted flat. This is the problem of a very small kitchen with awkward built-in fixtures. As Plan E shows, one corner of the small oblong is cut off by the larder. Shelves take up another corner, and two doors further cut up the wall space. The wall next the larder is occupied by a big gas storage-heater for hot water and the gas cooker. On the opposite wall, the low sink and draining-board have cupboards under. The remaining twelve inches are filled by a miniature dresser.

More working surface and easily get-at-able storage accommodation were required. The fourth short wall, with a bare four feet between door and corner shelves, was one place for a table or counter unit. A three-foot oblong-shaped marble-topped washstand, from which the back was removed, answers admirably. The back, reversed, makes a saucepan shelf, while hooks beneath take lids, soup ladles, cooking-spoons and similar impedimenta. The cupboards are roomy enough for mixing-bowl, basins and other cooking crockery, and the single drawer holds kitchen cutlery.

The little dresser takes the china not stored in the dining-room, while baking tins and casseroles go into the cupboard below, along with the housemaid's box. To provide an easily accessible home for dry goods, to save going to the deep-shelved larder, a small bookshelf has been fixed to the wall between dresser and plate-rack. Additional working surface is given by a flap-table fixed to the larder door. It's the only place where the wringer and the mincer can be screwed.

A big improvement could be made by gutting the side of the kitchen next the larder and installing more modern equipment. The water-heater, though efficient, is wasteful of space. The gas stove, owing to the placing of pipes, takes up more room than is necessary. With more modern equipment there would be room for a refrigerator and portable washing machine, too. An even better rearrangement would be to remove the existing sink and dresser and put in a complete sink unit, with washing machine, water-heater and refrigerator built in.

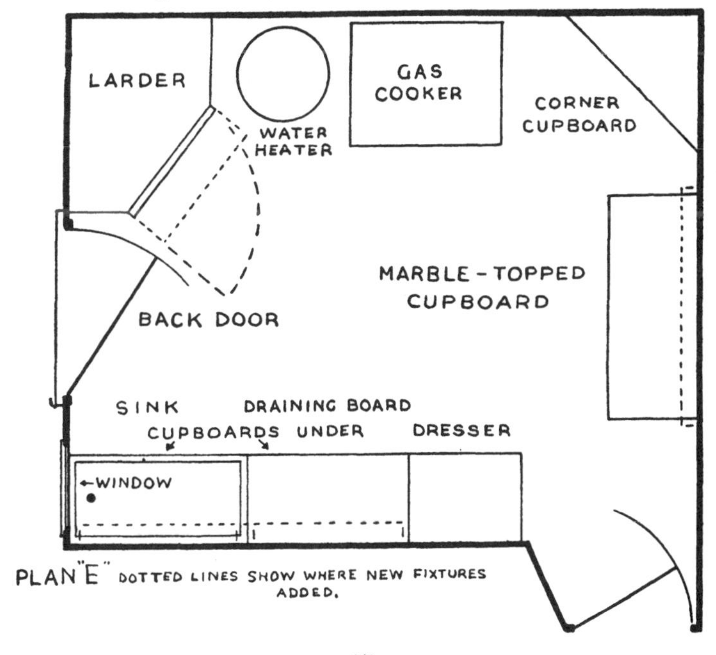

PLAN "E" DOTTED LINES SHOW WHERE NEW FIXTURES ADDED.

Such alterations would not be justified by the terms of the present lease, though they would be well worth while for an owner-occupier.

Your kitchen has quite different snags? Probably so, but these examples do show that even a little rearrangement can cut out quite a lot of work. It's always worth giving some thought to the matter.

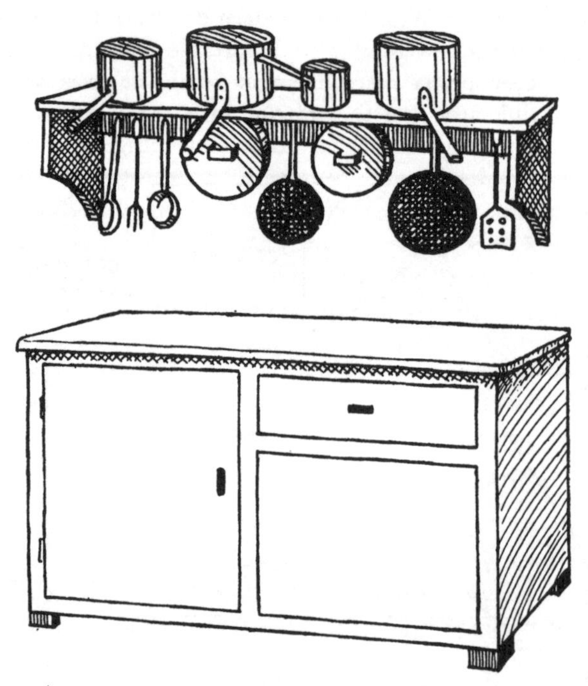

CONVERTED MARBLE-TOPPED WASHSTAND.

Chapter VI

THE DAILY ROUND

It's a remarkable woman who does not wake up some mornings with the thought "If only the same old round had not to be gone through." For, however you try to work it, beds have to be made, rooms tidied and dishes washed *every* day. And the disheartening part is that almost as soon as one has finished, it's time to start again. There's a good deal of satisfaction to be had from 'craft' jobs, such as washing and ironing, or polishing furniture, or even turning out a room. But the results obtained from the quick 'run round' are apt to be too fleeting to compensate for the time taken up.

But since the daily routine is a chore there's no escaping, the only sensible thing is to get through it in the most business-like way possible, using the head to save hands and feet.

BEGIN OVERNIGHT.

The best time to start is overnight! A sitting-room put straight before going to bed never has the sordid appearance next morning of the one left anyhow. Cushions that have been plumped out before their creases became set, chairs and covers straightened, ash-trays emptied, what a difference such things make. Yet a few minutes before turning-in isn't noticed or grudged.

If there is a fire to be cleared out and relaid, at least take out the scuttle ready for filling. Very often the man of the house will go further and get it ready for next day. At the same time the hod for the kitchen boiler should be recharged. Having to go out into the early morning chill to shovel up anthracite is a grim task.

So first of all decide what part of the daily round can be forestalled, and do what is necessary before going to bed.

DECIDE ON YOUR ORDER OF WORK.

Next, settle the order for the morning's tasks. If you live in a flat or a bungalow, with everything on one floor, you'll want a different approach from the classic one recommended for the house with up and downstairs. According to the latter, the downstairs is made presentable first, with priority given to the front of the house, where, if visitors were to call, they could be received.

What worries some who are planning the round for the first time is whether any work should be allotted to the pre-breakfast hour. The answer must depend on personal taste and habits. There's no doubt that early rising is a great help to the single-handed housewife, but some work well on an empty stomach, and some don't—there's no need to be hard and fast about it.

If, however, you want breakfast as soon as possible after scrambling out of bed, do plan your living so that you either eat the first meal of the day in the kitchen, or else in a room that you can make ready overnight. If you choose the latter, a quick dust will be all that is necessary before the meal, providing you've set the table ahead, and covered it with a cloth that can be just whipped off.

There is one chore, spared to those who have gas or electrically-heated hot-water supply, that should be coped with before breakfast, whatever one feels about the desirability of an early breaking of the fast. That is, riddling and refuelling the coke or anthracite boiler. How long this will take depends on the efficiency of the apparatus. The kind popular in small houses before the war tends to be a trifle temperamental. It may respond swiftly and need only a few minutes attention. On the other hand, if the fuel has got caked, or the boiler is nearing the time for its weekly clean out, fifteen minutes will go like a flash. Modern improved boilers are both cleaner and need less time spent on them. A clever wife induces her husband to regard the boiler as his special province! Whoever does it, it's worthwhile studying the particular model and learning all its vagaries and the treatment most likely to draw a quick response.

FIREPLACES FIRST.

Should you be of the school that likes to get going early, concentrate, after having done the boiler, on the sitting-room or lounge. The usual pre-breakfast task is the fire, if there is one to do. If ordinary house coal is burned, cleaning out the grate tends to be a grubby job, so cover chairs and settee with dust-sheets as far as possible. Take in with you dustpan and brush, blacklead brushes, if used, damp cloth and soapy cleaner, together with a couple of sheets of newspaper. The material for laying the fire will need a second journey.

Move back the curb or fender, roll up the hearth-rug and remove to one side. Put down your newspaper so that it comes well up to the hearth. The various types of grates have different movable and fixed parts, but the thing to do is to clear out the grate with as few movements, and raising as little dust as possible. Sweep up into the grate, and never out into the room, and don't forget to give the back of the chimney a brush down. After emptying the grate, re-lay it, and if necesary blacklead the front. Remove any marks from the tiled hearth with the cleanser, which can be a paste, powder or liquid.

While re-laying the fire, look over the hearth furniture, which, in your own interests, have as simple as possible, and preferably oxidised if of brass or copper. A daily dust should be sufficient, or at most a rub over with an impregnated cloth.

Try to have a cover for the pan in which you carry out the ashes, to save dust flying around. If cinders have to be sifted, take the pan straight out to the sieve or cinder rocker, cover immediately and leave. Use the sifted cinders the following day and bring in with the coals.

DOING THE ROOMS.

Fires done, you can go on to the sitting-rooms or the front porch and hall. For the front porch, a sweep or a damp mop should answer. Which order you decide on doing the downstairs rooms will depend on their layout. Outside porch, dining and sitting-rooms, then upstairs, is as good as any. After the upstairs rooms are finished, give the landing and stairs their quick once over, finishing up with the downstairs hall and kitchen. This order is quite optional. The important thing is to work out a convenient routine and follow it so that it becomes largely automatic.

When you begin tidying up the rooms, have your tools to hand. In the average room, with centre carpet and polished surround, you will need carpet sweeper, carpet brush for difficult-to-get-at corners, dusting mop and duster. For a room with a lot of polished floor, it may be worth while to use a floor polisher. It depends on the use given the rooms, and the time at your disposal. For dusting, some people like two dusters, one plain, one lightly impregnated with furniture oil. If there are glass-topped tables, take a damp cloth with you for a quick wipe over.

On coming into the room, take out any faded flowers or dirty ash-trays not removed overnight. Then use the carpet brush if necessary. Whether you dust or finish the floor next is a question of choice. Apart from the fact that any dust-raising jobs should be done first, the order doesn't really matter.

If you start with the dusting, begin at the left-hand side of the door, and holding your duster open and lightly crumpled in one hand, go quickly but methodically round the room, not forgetting tops of pictures and mirrors and the legs of chairs. With open bookshelves, wipe over the tops of books and round the sides. More thorough treatment must be reserved for the weekly turn-out.

From dusting one room, go straight on to the next on the same floor. Then preferably in the garden, otherwise in the kitchen, shake out the duster into the dustbin. After dusting, wipe over any soiled glass surfaces with the damp cloth.

Again beginning at one side and working carefully round, pass the dusting mop over the polished floors. Repeat the shaking-out process, taking care the dust *does* go into the bin and not over the room or garden. Try to have two mops, one in use, one spare. Then with regular shampooing the mops will keep fresh and do their job better.

Begin carpet sweeping at the end of the room away from the door. Move chairs and similar furniture out of the way first. Empty the sweeper before putting away.

Unless they have already been washed, do the breakfast dishes next, before going on to the upstairs rooms.

An alternative method is to put the kitchen straight immediately after breakfast; then do washing-up and sweep the floor before starting on the sitting-rooms. Both ways have their points. If the breakfast dishes are to be left, pile them up first, putting the porridge saucepan to soak, and the knives and forks in a jug of warm water. This cuts down the actual washing-up time.

Still another routine is the 'wet and dry jobs' one; particularly good for the all-on-one-floor house. This is the order: (1) pile the breakfast dishes; (2) make the beds; (3) dust and sweep all the rooms, also stairs if any, and hall; (4) sweep the kitchen; (5) 'wet' jobs follow, beginning with washing-up and going on to the lavatory and bathroom. Do any soiled paintwork or tiles that need a quick wipe over while you have the wet cloths handy.

BATHROOM AND LAVATORY.

Keep special cloths for the lavatory and see that they are rinsed and put to dry after use. Some people like to use the lavatory brush, with powder cleaner, as well as disinfectant, daily. The seat and pedestal will want wiping round and drying.

Which is the better order, bathroom and lavatory floors, or the respective basins and the bath? It rather depends whether one is working from cleaner to dirtier jobs, or the other way round. A linoleum-covered floor will probably need wiping with a special swab to take up damp patches, before it's gone over with the dusting mop and finished off with the polisher. A tiled floor will need a damp mop only. As the floor will still be wet after mopping, in this case, make it the last job in the room.

See that a suitable cloth, a piece of old towelling for instance, and cleaner is kept in a bathroom cupboard, so that there is no excuse for anyone using the bath not wiping it round afterwards.

This will lighten the daily clean; so will using a water softener in the bath. Even so, some attention will be necessary. A damp cloth dipped into liquid soap substitute may be sufficient to take off any marks. On the other hand, powder or paste cleaner, and a good hard rub may be called for. Experiment as to which proves most satisfactory for your particular kind of bath. After removing marks—and remember, a damp, not a wet cloth—swill round with clear water and dry with fresh cloth. The lavatory basin will need the same treatment, though a slightly sketchier one usually suffices. Wipe over mirrors, chromium taps and shelves with a damp cloth, and that's that.

BEDMAKING.

Bedmaking can be quite a pleasant interlude from the dusting and sweeping. Also it has the advantage of stretching the muscles without undue exertion. Whether you follow a 'hospital bed' method, with every covering punctiliously smoothed and tightly tucked in with mitred corners, or a more casual style, is a question of taste. To some people it's misery if folds are not left in the sheets to allow for easy turning and movement in bed.

But do see that every bed is stripped and aired, with the bedroom window opened at the bottom, before breakfast. Charge the last one to leave the bedroom with this little duty. Try, too, to get whoever does it to place the clothes fairly near, perhaps over a clothes-horse or chair, in the order in which they will be replaced. This saves precious minutes, and steps.

WASHING-UP.

Washing-up is a task regarded with particular horror by many, yet really it needn't be so bad. During the war, when soap was too scarce to allow of it being used in the washing-up bowl, it was certainly harder, but with the coming of the liquid soap substitute one can luxuriate in nice sudsy water. Providing the latter is hot, and you are armed with a good mop, dish-cloth, bottle brush, saucepan brush, and fine steel wool for obstinate cases, you can sail right ahead.

Before beginning on a single cup, do scrape all food remnants off the plates, empty tea-leaves and cups, and pile everything up, ready to hand, with the least soiled and less greasy things placed so that they will be washed first. Put cold water in jugs or basins that have had milk or a starchy substance, such as flour or cornflour, in them. Soak greasy things in hot water. Begin on the glass or the silver and cutlery. Then do the china in order; finally pans and cooking utensils, which will thus have had more time to soak. For saucepans, an inexpensive saucepan brush, made from vegetable 'bristles' bound together with copper wire, proves most satisfactory. It can't hurt the pans, and unless fat is burnt on, or the pan discoloured, it will do the job. When aluminium saucepans are scorched, very fine steel wool and pure soap are best. Be sure to rinse very well, else a nasty black mark will come off on to the tea-towel. Don't use the steel wool for the insides of saucepans if it can be avoided. For the outsides, soap is not necessary. Scouring powder will usually get marks off enamel pans. Always try long soaking rather than drastic cleaning. When the brush is not sufficient for caked-on baking tins, use the fine steel wool.

If you have a plate-rack, which is a time-saver the single-handed housewife should not be without, use it to the full. When you begin on the drying-up, leave the things in the rack until last. They will only need a wipe round the edge. Soap substitute in the washing-up bowl leaves the china looking bright and unsmeared. If soap, ammonia powder, or, worst of all, soda, has been used to soften the water, the crockery should be rinsed before drying, else smears are likely.

Bedmaking, breakfast dishes and tidying the kitchen; dusting and sweeping the sitting-rooms, bedrooms, stairs, passage and porch; riddling the boiler and cleaning out the fire; putting to rights the lavatory and bathroom—there, in greater or less detail, is the inescapable morning routine. It may take anything from an hour in a small flat, to two or more in a house, depending on the amount to be done and the speed of working.

Although on occasion some duties will have to be scamped, there's not much that can be omitted altogether. A certain lightening will come from the fact that the rooms having their weekly clean can be left out from the morning tidying. Some days, too, you'll vary the order. On the whole, it's a good plan to get shipshape before setting out on the shopping, but there are times when this just can't be done. If, too, small children have to be taken to school, it's better to carry straight on with the shopping. Every one must just work out what is most practical in the particular circumstances; keeping in mind that though method is a good thing, being a slave of the house is not. A pinch of common sense goes a long way!

Chapter VII

THE WEEKLY CLEANING

TO THE casual visitor it all looks charming. Everything is tidy, the flowers are fresh. There's no obvious dust on furniture or floors. To you, however, your home presents a very different appearance. Giving the sitting-room the usual swift 'do' this morning you noticed that the mirrors seemed dull, that the little chandelier, your pride and joy, didn't sparkle with its accustomed brightness.

When you moved some books, marks on the shelves where each one had rested caught your eye. In the bedroom, the window sill and frames seem to attract great smudges of dirt on the white paint almost every other day, while the way the rest of the paint gets soiled is uncanny.

So there it is. Mother was not so far wrong when she insisted that all the rooms must be 'turned out' every week. Mother, however, had regular help. She did the cooking herself and she had a washer-woman in weekly so that the maid could concentrate on housework alone. You must devote one morning a week at least to the washing you daren't entrust to the laundry. One day you must concentrate on cooking to the exclusion of all else. Saturday morning you want to be as free as possible, so that you are clear by lunch-time when your husband comes home. Sunday is reserved, too. That means there are three days only when you can make house cleaning your main concern. So you must divide up what has to be done over the three days.

Where shall we begin? Only by practice can you determine which rooms take longest, just how much can be achieved in the time allotted. But, as a starting point, let's say sitting-rooms one day, bedrooms the next, hall, stairs, passages, bathroom and lavatory the third. The kitchen can probably be left until Friday, after the baking is done. When deciding on the order, try to do adjacent rooms at one time, and to work in a light job with a heavier one. Once you've decided on a plan, stick to it!

COLLECT YOUR TOOLS.

Supposing it's the day for the sitting-rooms. First check over your tools. For the *floors*; vacuum cleaner or carpet brush, dustpan and sweeper, together with floor polish, cloth for putting on, and another for rubbing up, unless you have a long-handled floor polisher. *Furniture* needs furniture cream or wax polish, again with a special cloth, as well as the soft duster that can be used for a variety of polishing jobs. French-polished mahogany or walnut you may prefer to leather over with a damp chamois to remove any dirt, and then polish with the cloth only.

Upholstery gets dusty, so a little whisk brush, or better still, a hand vacuum, or special attachment to the large vacuum cleaner, is needed. *Mirrors, picture glasses* and *chandelier drops* call for a liquid window or mirror cleaner, again with cloth. Alternatively, use linen scrim, a chamois and a little methylated spirits. A white paste cleaner does the best job of removing marks and generally freshening window sills and frames, skirting boards, doors and other *paintwork*. *Hearth tiles* can be rubbed up with floor polish or special tile cleaner. If there is a *picture rail*, a long-handled dusting brush is wanted. It's good for the top of the doors, too. And of course you need dust-sheets. Lastly, ornamental *silver*, *copper* or *brass* will need the appropriate kind of metal cleaner.

HAVE A HOUSEMAID'S BOX.

Store all cleaning materials in a special box, preferably one with a handle that can be easily carried around. Stand it on a sheet of newspaper in the room where you are working, and put back each cleaner as finished with. It's the sign of a slovenly worker to leave jars and tins around! Never carelessly put them down on a polished surface. Only metal cleaners are best left in the kitchen, and the articles to be cleaned brought out. In fact, you may prefer to regard metal cleaning as a job on its own, and do everything in the house one day a week, or fortnight, or even once a month, according to the time to be spared.

One of the points that the beginner tends to overlook is the quantity of cleaning cloths necessary. Different polishes must be put on with their own piece of rag, if dirt is not to be carried from one article to another. So never throw away old underwear, tea-towels, sheets or shirts, or, in fact, anything that can possibly be pressed into service for use as cleaning or polishing rags. Some cloths can be washed out easily each week, such as those used for paintwork, also leathers and scrim. Others that are impregnated with furniture or floor polish, for example, are not worth the soap and the trouble. Use for a few weeks until too grubby, and then discard. Incidentally, old socks and other soft woolly materials are fine for floor flannels and polishers.

TURNING OUT THE SITTING-ROOM.

But let's get down to the work. There's one joy about turning out a room, the results do show. We all have our pet ways of working, but the order after clearing the decks and making ready should be as follows: (1) take up loose dust; (2) detailed cleaning and polishing; (3) restore order.

1. Deal with Loose Dust.

If you have a nice large hall, bring out small chairs and tables from the sitting-room, dusting them as you do so. Otherwise, dust and push them to one side of the room where they can be covered with a dust-sheet. Cover settee and upholstered chairs, too. If the whisk brush is to be used on upholstery, do it before covering up. When you have to use a carpet brush on the floor, it's as well to do that first as it's bound to raise the dust somewhat. Vacuuming can well be left until later.

Next go round the top of door and picture rail or cornice with the long-handled brush. Then use the duster in the ordinary way to remove surface dust from furniture. Give the curtains a brush with the whisk, or shake lightly. If the vacuum attachment, or a hand cleaner, is being used for the upholstery, the curtains can have a turn at the same time. Loop up curtains carefully, so that the floor is cleared and the window left free. If window frames are to be wiped over, and the insides of windows cleaned, net curtains must be taken down or drawn back out of the way. Take off standard-lamp shades and brush or vacuum.

Collect any ornaments from mantelpiece or tables and take outside the room, place carefully in a big basket or lay on the settee under the dust-cover. Give them a dust as you do this. China will need a wipe with a damp cloth every so often. Other *objets d'art* must be cared for according to their kind. Unless you have only a few books, they will have to be taken out from the shelves and dusted individually a few at a time. One section one week, another the next, and so on. It's best to do this while engaged on polishing the furniture, then the bookshelf can be given a rub up as the books are removed.

Now carpets. Take out small rugs for a shake, then use the vacuum cleaner. Do any upholstery that you feel needs it, also the curtains.

2. Mirrors, Paintwork, Furniture, Floor Surrounds.

With the room clear and all the dusty operations finished, it doesn't matter greatly what you do next. It might be the mirrors and picture glasses, with the insides of the windows. Apply the special liquid cleaner, or go over them with a dampened chamois leather. Leave to dry. Tackle the paintwork next. In your daily dusting you will probably have noticed any grubby marks or smears. Rub these gently with a damp cloth and a little white paste cleaner. The window sill and frame may want washing all over. In which case, have a special cloth if you don't want your paint-cleaning one to become badly soiled. While the paint is drying, go over the mirrors etc., taking off the now dry polish and giving a rub up. If you used a chamois, polish with scrim. Be sure to stand away from the glass to make certain there are no smears. Then give the paintwork a polish with a soft duster, or, if you've time, apply a little white furniture cream to it.

The rule for using furniture cream, or polish of any kind, is: very little of it, but a lot of rubbing, or elbow grease as it used to be called. If there are any dirty marks or stains on furniture it's better to remove them with a cloth wrung out in soapy water first. But if the rule of only a little polish is followed, this shouldn't be necessary. Furniture with a fairly high polish of its own responds best to furniture cream, unless it is simply leathered, dried and rubbed up with a soft cloth. Wax-polished oak, pine or whitewood can be treated with colourless wax polish.

What remains? The floor surrounds must be polished. Unless the room is large, it's worth squatting down and putting on the polish by hand. Use it sparingly, rub in well, and leave to dry before polishing up. For the latter, a long-handled polisher is useful. You can buy hand polishers with a brush one side, intended for applying the polish, and a pad for rubbing up on the other. In many ways, however, it's still better to put on the polish with a cloth and leave the brush for the days when a rub up, but not fresh polish, is required. Otherwise, it tends to get clogged with polish. Some electric polishers apply polish, too.

3. Finishing Touches.

While the surrounds are drying, polish the hearth tiles. For glazed ones, colourless wax polish is excellent. For red, unglazed ones, a special tile polish is sold. Rub up the floor surround last of all. Put back the furniture and ornaments in position, and remove cleaning gear. As you give a final proud glance you can feel that the room shouldn't need more than the daily flick over for the next week.

More likely than not, that full programme may not be possible each week. In that case, portion out the various operations over, say, a month. One week do the chandelier, insides of windows if necessary, and the picture glasses. The next, leave them, but give the furniture a good polish. The third, concentrate on upholstery, lamp shades and heavy curtains. The fourth, see that silver, copper, brass or other ornaments have special care. Do a little paintwork each week if possible, should it be light and show the dirt. As for mirrors, try to polish them each week, as they look sad when dull. The floor needs regular treatment, too, as it is bound to get most wear, but if time is short on occasion, cut out the polishing, give a rub up with the polisher and vacuum the carpets.

You will want roughly the same tools and method for the dining-room as the sitting-room, but the former, being usually less furnished and less used, shouldn't need nearly as much work.

BEDROOMS.

How long the bedrooms will take depends largely upon the amount of built-in furniture. In a modern room, with flush-doored fixtures carried up to the ceiling, there won't be much more to it than moving out the beds, taking the various articles from the dressing-table, polishing the few pieces of furniture and the mirrors and doing the floor. Where, however, there are several chests of drawers, wardrobes and cupboards of assorted heights, some coming right down to the floor and others with feet and legs that make it difficult to reach underneath them, it can be a full morning's work.

Whatever the type of room, the beds should be moved out so that the floor beneath can be thoroughly gone over. This is particularly important with an interior-spring divan, which, coming almost to the floor, can't be swept under like an ordinary bed. Before moving beds, lift up the valance or bedspread and fold it back over the bed. If you have a fitted divan cover that comes to the floor, take it off. Then cover completely with a dust-sheet.

After this preliminary, get rid of loose dust. Run the long-handled brush over the top of cupboards and door, and your duster over lower furniture surfaces. Give the pendant lamp shades a dust, too. It's rather shaming the amount of dust a whisk brush will discover if they're left for more than a couple of weeks.

Unless the room is sparsely furnished, it will probably be easier to do the rest in two parts. When the beds are moved, don't be surprised to see a large amount of fluff. Get this up straight away. If carpeted, use the vacuum cleaner. If a polished wood or linoleum floor, a wash over, after a preliminary sweeping, is freshening.

Small movable chests of drawers or cupboards that come flush down to the floor should be moved out in rotation so that the floor may be attended to. Dust won't have penetrated underneath as a rule, but an awkward-to-get-at rim all round the edge is common. Leave any washed floors to dry before polishing, and in the meanwhile give the furniture a rub up. Then finish the floor and move the beds back.

The dressing-table and the window will most likely be in the second half of the room. Strip the former of its furnishings and put them carefully on the bed. Do the second half of the floor in the same way as the first. Then polish the rest of the furniture or do the mirrors. Order is immaterial. Any time over can be given to removing marks from the paintwork. As bedroom windows tend to be open at all times, the frames and sill often get very grubby. Bedroom curtains are usually of the light washable kind; but if you favour heavier draperies, go over with a whisk brush, or the hand vacuum, or attachment to the big cleaner, as often as possible.

CORRIDORS.

Let's polish off the corridors, stairs, hall and front porch next. If you have a house, begin upstairs with the corridors. Dust any pictures extra carefully, and don't forget that ornamental vases and such like want attention, too. Take up the dust, and then treat floors according to kind, brushing or using the vacuum cleaner on rugs or carpets, polishing wood or linoleum. Take care not to give too much of a shine where there are loose rugs, it's dangerous.

Skirting boards next. Have your paint cleaner and damp cloth ready. If they are polished, not painted, use the furniture polish or cream instead. A little regular care and the job is quickly done. Now on to the stairs.

STAIRS.

If you can acquire a little hand vacuum, you will find it cuts down the time necessary for this particular job very agreeably. Without one, or a special attachment to the large vacuum, it means a stiff brush and dust-pan for the carpet. Brush down each individual stair; then, starting at the top again, do the sides with paint cleaner or polish, according to the finish. Finally, a rub up to the banisters, and that's that. If you're a bit ahead some weeks, slip out the stair rods or clips. This means a more thorough clean to the carpet and an opportunity to give the rods themselves a polish. Don't have brass rods unless they're lacquered. The extra work occasioned is not worth while.

FRONT HALL.

The amount of traffic will determine the treatment for the front hall. In a flat proceed as if you were doing the floor of a room. Where there are muddy feet in and out of the garden, a wash over will probably be necessary for linoleum or tiles. Avoid scrubbing for the sake of the floor as well as that of your knees. It's better to use a damp mop daily, and then to wash over with a soft flannel when really necessary, rather than to go all out with a scrubbing brush once a week. Again be careful with the polish under rugs. Slippery floors can cause bad accidents.

Deal with ornaments, paintwork, furniture, mirrors, etc., in the hall as you would if doing a room, portioning out over several weeks if necessary. If a trolley is pushed up and down, skirting boards get a good deal of wear, so wipe over each week if the paint is light and shows marks.

FRONT DOOR, PORCH . . .

The front door and porch, with any outside steps, can take up far too much time if allowed to. If, for instance, the door-knocker, letter-box and so forth are of brass that tarnishes quickly, consider having them replaced by chromium ones. If these would look out of place, what about enamelling black the existing set? It's not difficult to do at home. Unscrew, rub down with emery paper, and give several coats of paint or enamel, allowing to dry in between. For the door itself, a dust and a little polishing should be sufficient.

. . . AND STEPS.

Ideally, a tiled porch floor should be polished. Remove any muddy marks with a damp cloth, or wash over if absolutely necessary, leave to dry, then polish as usual. If, however, this chore is just one too many, cut out the polishing and simply wash over with a self-wringing mop each day, using enough water to swill down.

Outside steps can be treated similarly, though a weekly scrub will improve their look. If you feel this must be done, invest in a long-handled scrubber and avoid the knee drill.

LAVATORY . . .

So on to the lavatories and bathrooms. Don't be squeamish about the former. It's a much simpler job than you might think, if you've never done it. Overnight, sprinkle the pan with a special lavatory cleaner and flush out in the morning. For the cleaning proper, sprinkle the bowl with an ordinary scouring powder, pour in some really hot water, in which a handful of washing soda has been dissolved, and scrub round with the lavatory brush. Flush, and then, using your special cloth, wipe all round the inside of the bowl carefully. Next do the outside, not forgetting the underside of the seat. Dry carefully. A polish to the seat woodwork gives the finishing touch.

Leave the lavatory brush in a hot soda solution for a few minutes, rinse well and hang out to dry. If a lavatory-brush container is used, give this a wash out with the hot soda water before returning the brush.

For a discoloured lavatory bowl, make up a solution of any of the commercial bleaches sold for clothes washing, sinks, lavatories, and so forth, and leave in the bowl for as long as possible before washing round with the brush. Alternatively, use a mild solution of spirits of salts. But avoid such drastic measures if possible. Strong chemicals can't help but do damage to the glaze.

Before leaving the lavatory, dust round carefully, not forgetting the top of the cistern. Deal with any marks on the walls, and, if you have time, go over the skirting board. Wipe or wash over the floor as necessary, and polish.

. . . AND BATHROOM.

How long the bathroom takes will depend largely upon the efficiency of the daily 'do'. Give the bath a rather more careful scrutiny than you have time for on ordinary days. The new soap substitute in tablet form is efficient for getting off obstinate marks made by soap scum and hard water. Use paste cleaner or scouring powder if preferred. Any rust marks, made by a dripping tap, may need just a drop or two of vinegar on a damp cloth. Be careful to rub the mark only, else the acid will take the gloss off the bath.

Next, clear any shelves and wash them over, or, if of glass, clean with mirror polish while doing the mirrors. Give the taps a wipe with a damp cloth and a polish with a dry one. Use the damp cloth, with a little paint cleaner if necessary, for taking splash marks off the walls. Tiles will need a wipe over finished by a polish.

The damp cloth will constantly need rinsing out, so have some warm water in the lavatory basin and leave cleaning that until the rest is done. When all looks fresh and gleaming, wipe over the floor and polish carefully, remembering that polish should be left to dry before the final rub up.

Chapter VIII

MORE WEEKLY CLEANING

SINCE the kitchen is your workshop, you'll be perpetually tidying it up; giving the floor a sweep, and wiping down the dresser or working surfaces. In spite of this, the room will need a weekly clean. Also, there are various other cleaning jobs associated with the kitchen that must be worked into the rota. If you're wise, you'll not attempt them all at once.

Turning out the larder, for instance, is logically done the same day as the main grocery order comes. Defrosting the refrigerator can well be dealt with then, too. Bleaching the sink follows well on Monday's wash, for the bleach used for the tea-towels can do double duty. Cleaning the stove should, perhaps, come after baking, but as there is usually the kitchen to clear up and cooking utensils to wash it may be better to leave it for a slack hour some other time in the week.

Doing the kitchen is in many households Friday's task, after the weekly cake-making. This timing has the advantage of leaving the kitchen bright for the weekend, though unless care is used, Sunday's dinner may leave its mark on floor and stove. However, that's one of the housewife's worst banes—the results of her labour never show for long!

TURNING OUT THE LARDER.

This does not involve taking out all your stock of dry goods and cans, though it's as well to check these through each week before making out the grocery list. All perishables should come out. Clear a space on a table or cupboard top in a cool part of the kitchen for them. As everything is brought out in turn, notice whether any remainders should be placed on fresh dishes, fats rewrapped or dripping reclarified.

When the larder is clear, wipe down the shelves, using, if necessary, a little white paste cleaner or liquid soap substitute to remove any marks. If you have separate tiles or enamel trays in the larder, take out and wash carefully, paying particular attention to drying, else moisture will condense under the tiles when they are replaced. Give the window frame a wipe over too, but don't use your best paint cloth, for it will probably be turned black with the smuts that blow in. A larder needs to be airy, but gauze will not keep out dirt!

When replacing the food, see that the new supplies go at the back and the first-bought in the front, so that it will be used up first. In summer-time at least, when flies are about, cover over all the perishables with clean butter muslin, unless you have a meat safe in the larder to take them.

CLEANING THE KITCHEN SINK.

Every day after washing-up, it's sensible to wash both inside and out of the washing-up bowl, and to give the same attention to the sink, too. Often, though, with the clock racing on, this routine will be somewhat hurried, so a weekly special clean is needed. For removing grease the new liquid soap substitute is quick and successful. Dip the cloth into a little hot water containing a tablespoonful of the soap substitute and wipe round sink, bowl and sink tidy. For any bad grease spots, use a little 'neat' liquid on the cloth. Give the taps a wipe over with the same cloth and polish with a dry one. Although freeing the sink from grease, this treatment will not remove stains.

For a non-metal sink, use a commercial bleach. Pour in enough solution, of the same kind as used for the lavatory bowl and for bleaching tea-cloths, to cover the bottom. Leave for as long as possible, then swill round, and rinse thoroughly. If the solution is at all strong, use a mop; or wear rubber gloves if your hands are sensitive. It's better, however, to use the mildest strength that will do the job. Finish by pouring a little disinfectant down the pipe. Fine steel wool and soap do the best job with aluminium, while stainless steel, as its name implies, needs least care of all. For a special finish, use a little powdered whitening.

HOW TO CARE FOR THE COOKER.

Not to wipe over both the hotplates and the oven after using the stove is to make work. All the same, although such first-aid treatment will avoid the necessity of drastic periodic cleaning, a little more is necessary every so often if the cooker is to function at its best.

For a gas stove, remove the boiling-plates, noting the order. Then either scrub them with a stiff brush in hot soda water, taking care that the jets are freed from grease, or use the liquid soap substitute. Although much milder and pleasanter to use, this kind of preparation is so effective with grease that it will do the job equally well. Wipe down the non-movable parts of the top of the stove with a hot damp cloth, again using the soap substitute, or, alternatively, scouring powder. Fine steel wool will remove any obstinate marks.

How much attention is needed will depend largely upon whether you are the fortunate possessor of a modern, new stove, or have an older, less labour-saving model. In either case, regular cleanliness pays!

Take out the oven shelves and immerse in the hot soda water, or hot water with the liquid soap substitute. Treat the inside of the oven as the top of the stove. Then dry the shelves and replace. Finish by doing the enamel part of the outside either with the soap substitute or with a paste cleaner. Don't forget the porcelain tray on top of the oven and the grill-pan.

If this simple routine is followed regularly, there will never be need for caustic cleaners, neither will your oven belch forth acrid fumes caused by deposits of burned grease.

With an electric cooker, none of the movable parts must be put in water. They may be wiped over with a damp cloth, but it is dangerous to allow water to come into contact with the element. Otherwise the cleaning method is much the same as with a gas cooker. Most electric companies supply explicit directions for cleaning their stoves. These should be followed exactly.

Solid-fuel stoves have flues to be cleaned and, with oil stoves, lamps must be carefully looked to. Otherwise the routine follows the same general lines as detailed above. Again, let the maker's instructions be your guide in the matter.

THE REFRIGERATOR.

After the golden rule of 'follow the maker's instructions for defrosting the refrigerator' has been complied with, wash out the inside of the cabinet with warm water to which you have added a teaspoonful of bicarbonate of soda, not ordinary washing soda.

Stove, sink, larder and refrigerator dealt with, what else is there in the kitchen? Only too much, if you allow your eye to wander; but take it easily! Nothing else beyond the floor need be done every week. For the rest, it's best to divide tidying up the various cupboards and stores, going over the paintwork, of which there is a lot in most modern kitchens, washing down open dressers and their contents, and giving the saucepans and kettles an extra polish, into four parts. Try to do one job, or a section of the cupboards, once a month in rotation.

SAUCEPANS.

For aluminium saucepans, give the outsides a burnish with a little fine steel wool, using it dry. A similar treatment, but with soap used on the moistened wool, will remove stains from the outside of enamel pans. Go carefully, though.

THE FLOOR.

The kitchen floor does get a lot of wear, so you may feel that it should be washed over each week. Unless it is badly stained and muddy, just use a damp cloth on any marks, and then rely on the polish to clean. Apply the polish carefully, leave to dry, and then rub up vigorously.

If the floor is tiled, wash over with a self-wringing mop or a damp cloth. If liked, polish lightly, but be sparing with the polish.

METAL CLEANING.

Metal cleaning is a periodic job, best tackled in the seclusion of the kitchen or utility room, so let's have a look at it now. First thing to remember is that the various metals require quite different treatment.

For *brass* and *copper* use any of the special metal polish sold, e.g. Bluebell or Brasso, or an impregnated wool, such as Duraglit. *Never* use metal polish on goods with an oxydised or lacquered finish. It is fatal. A rub up with a soft cloth is all that is necessary.

Chromium plating, too, is ruined by the application of metal polish. A special liquid cleaner, e.g. Windolene, good for mirrors and windows, can also be used for chromium, if liked.

For *silver* and *silver plate* you have a choice. There are good proprietary liquid and powder cleaners of the rouge and whitening types, and also impregnated wool for a quick rub up. If preferred, precipitated whitening, moistened with a drop of methylated spirit or household ammonia, is good. To precipitate whitening, tie loosely in a muslin bag, put the bag in a basin and cover with cold water. Shake the bag vigorously so that the powder passes through the muslin. Leave overnight. Next day, the water must be poured off and the deposit of whitening in the basin left in a warm place to dry.

Precipitated whitening, moistened with a drop of sweet oil, is the safe cleaner for *old pewter*. Alternatively, rub up with a soft duster.

There is a quick method for *table silver* or *plate*. The equipment needed is an old aluminium saucepan, or a piece of aluminium, such as an old sink-tidy. Whatever is used must be kept for this purpose alone. Half fill the saucepan with water. Bring to the boil, then add washing soda in the proportion of one ounce of soda to two quarts of water. If using a piece of aluminium, not a saucepan, put this in any old saucepan with the same soda solution. Put in your knives and forks, leave for a moment and lift out, using tongs so that your fingers aren't burned. Wash in soapy water and dry carefully. All tarnish will be gone and the tableware will look soft and gleaming.

With the single exception of this 'electrolytic' method, as it is called, all metal cleaning is a dirty job. So cover your table with a thick sheet of newspaper, and wear old gloves. It's a good plan to keep all the equipment in a box. It should contain the appropriate polishes; old rags for applying the polish, and soft flannelly ones, or flannelette dusters, for rubbing up; a chamois leather and a silver brush.

Having collected all the metal and plate in need of attention, you can get going. Apply polish to several articles of a kind and allow to dry before rubbing up. Any filigree work, or chasing on silver, will need the brush to get the dried polish out of the crevices. Finally polish with a chamois leather, taking care to run lengthwise rather than crosswise, but, in any case, not with a circular motion. Any table silver cleaned this way needs washing in soapy water and carefully drying before use. 'Best' silver should be wrapped away in soft baize cloth. If cleaned after use, a quick refresher with the special wool impregnated with plate powder should be all that is necessary when next brought out.

Chapter IX

SPRING-CLEANING

THE BRIDE, looking at her new home, where everything sparkles or shines, is apt to think scornfully of her mother's intensive spring-cleans. Then the whole place was turned topsy-turvy and a regime of all-cold meals prevailed, while father talked darkly of going to his club and staying there. Nothing of that kind will ever disturb the serenity of *her* home life she swears.

Certainly, with comparatively few possessions, and most of them new, an intelligent housewife who cares for her home herself won't need to undertake very extensive spring-cleaning. As the years go on, and the home at the same time gets shabbier and more crowded, a good turn-out, once a year at least, seems imperative. All the same, there's no need to make a misery of it. Plan the work, do only at one time what can be got through without undue fatigue, and don't think that everything must be crowded into one hectic week.

But even when the decision is made to do one room this week, and one the next, there's no doubt that when the job is actually under way, a good deal has to be crammed into a comparatively short time. No one wants to have a room out of action for more than a day, if it can be avoided. In the circumstances, get as much as possible of the preliminary work done ahead, and rope in some help.

GET THE FAMILY TO HELP . . .

The annual refurbishing is surely an event in which the family can be expected to lend a hand. Get your husband to take over the vetting of equipment. Electric-light and power cords get frayed, for instance, and the vacuum cleaner will benefit from an overhaul. If he is anything of a handyman, much persuasion should not be needed to get him to embark on distempering or painting. Taking down and putting up curtains and such-like awkward jobs will not appeal to him, but with luck he'll rally round if approached diplomatically.

When the family grows bigger, teach the children to play their part. Even youngsters can learn to tidy their own toy cupboards or their special chest of drawers. It will help them to value their possessions if they have to take care of them.

. . . OR TEAM UP WITH A FRIEND.

Such help will be valuable, but it will still leave a pretty heavy day's work on your shoulders, unless you can team up with a friend in a similar position. You will, of course, return the compliment and give her a hand in turn. Two working together can swing along and get through a lot without much fatigue, providing, of course, that both know what to do and how to proceed. The routine to follow won't alter materially whether you work singly or in pairs, so, before beginning, it's worthwhile jotting down just what has to be done.

PLAN AROUND THE SWEEP'S VISIT . . .

If you have solid-fuel fires, and don't forget the kitchen boiler, engaging the sweep comes first. It may be necessary to book some time ahead, but, as you won't want his visit until fires are finished for the year, it's better that he should come later, rather than earlier than you wished. His visit will determine when the rooms with fires have to be tackled. When his call is timed for first thing in the morning, the room can be dismantled as far as possible overnight. Pictures and mirrors should be taken down, also curtains; ornaments removed, rugs rolled up. Everything left in the room must, of course, be well covered up. Then, after he has gone and the dust-sheets are removed, you can get straight on with your part.

While the sweep has been busy, you will have had an opportunity of washing the china, cleaning mirrors and picture glasses, shampooing the rugs, or getting on with any of the spring-cleaning tasks that are best tackled outside the room.

. . . OR THAT OF THE DECORATORS.

Similarly, if the decorators are coming in, organise the turning out round their stay. For instance, if the bedroom is to be distempered and painted one week, you could well decide to get the chests of drawers and wardrobes turned out the previous one. Immediately before the men come, the walls will have to be cleared and curtains taken down. The dressing-table furnishings will be safer outside, while the mattress can be vacuumed as well as the rugs.

As with the sweep's visit, you can get on with a good deal outside the room while the workmen are busy in it.

With the work thus dealt with in sections, there won't be a great deal to do when the men have gone. The floor will want a specially good clean, likewise the furniture. After that, nothing remains but to put back everything in place, hang fresh curtains, put on a summery bedspread, and admire the scene.

SPRING-CLEANING THE BEDROOM.

Supposing this year there is no decorating to be done in the bedroom? The whole job will fall on you, but you can make your own time-table. The following is the order.

Clear out and make ready all cupboards and drawers, taking one piece of furniture at a time. Give the insides a soap-and-water scrub, adding a little pleasant-smelling disinfectant to the water if you like. Leave to dry. While the woodwork is thus airing, tidy the contents. Unless you have plenty of drawer and cupboard space it's a good plan to pack away woollies and heavy winter clothes. This serves two purposes. It leaves room without crushing for summery attire, and enables you to give the rest an anti-moth treatment. How to do this is explained later in this chapter, on p. 84. If you live in a centrally heated flat it's advisable to spray all the insides of furniture with D.D.T. anti-moth insecticide before replacing the contents. In any case, line drawers and cupboards with fresh paper before clothes are put back.

Next, take down curtains, preparatory to washing or sending to the cleaners. If there is dressing-table drapery, dismantle this too, with any other soft furnishings, such as mats on chests of drawers.

Turning out drawers and cupboards can, of course, be spread over as most convenient, but don't strip the windows until the day before you're starting on the cleaning proper, and only then if you have blinds.

Another preliminary that, given time, can well be done ahead is the treatment of furniture for marks made by perfume or grease. Or deal with an isolated stain, such as an inkspot on the carpet. Leave all-over treatment until the main cleaning has been done. The best way to remove various types of stains is explained on pp. 85–7.

Strip, instead of making, the bed on the, let us hope, sunny day on which the room is to be done. If different sets of bedclothes are used for winter and summer, put aside the blankets and down quilt for washing or dry-cleaning. Otherwise take out of doors for an airing. It used to be considered the thing to take the mattress out of doors, too. That's fine if you have a helper and it's not a big interior-spring affair. On the whole, treatment has to be done in the room. If you have a vacuum cleaner, use that, on both sides of the mattress. Otherwise, try to drape your mattress over the window sill in the continental manner, to air. Give it a beat, too. When you've got it back, cover with a dust-sheet.

Take as much furniture as possible out of the room. Brush well any upholstered things, or go over them with the vacuum cleaner, using the appropriate attachment. The rest must be moved from the walls to the centre of the room and covered up. Take down pictures and remove ornaments. Collect these in a clothes-basket or tray and take to the kitchen for washing.

If rugs or carpets are not fastened down, vacuum clean on both sides. This is a precaution against moths. Then roll up and take out to air. If vacuuming is not possible, beat and brush in the garden. When the carpet is close fitted or tacked down, leave the cleaning until later, unless a carpet brush, that will raise the dust, has to be used.

Next give the walls and ceiling your attention, using the long-handled cornice brush. India-rubber or a piece of bread will often take out marks on wallpaper or distemper. The latter *can* be lightly washed down; but go very carefully, else the distemper will come off with the dirt.

Treat paintwork next. If this has been kept in reasonable order each week, it won't need much attention; but now is the time to make up for any neglect. As you will want to go round, have a pail of warm, softened water, as well as paste cleaner and wet and dry cloths. *Don't* use a brush. Enthusiastic novices have been known to *scrub* paintwork, with disastrous results to the paint!

If the floor is of polished wood or linoleum, give it a wash over with soap and water, or even a scrub, depending on condition. While it is drying, ornaments can be washed in the kitchen, mirrors and pictures cleaned and the frames rubbed up with a little furniture cream.

At this stage, if you haven't already had a break, stop and have a quick lunch.

Afterwards, vacuum any tacked-down carpet that hasn't already been dealt with. If the carpet is marked, or just has a greyed look all over, give it a shampoo. You may have to defer this until another day, but it all comes into the spring-cleaning, so here's the way to go about it.

Either use a good brand of carpet soap, a soap jelly, or a liquid soapless cleanser. Provide yourself with two bowls of water, a soft nail brush or a firm cloth and a second cloth for rinsing. Then, taking a square foot or two at a time, go over the carpet in sections. Use the smallest amount of water possible. Rub and rinse each section, using a wrung-out cloth for the latter, before going on to the next. Take care that each new portion overlaps the last to avoid a hard line. Rub as dry as possible. Of course, if you are using a proprietary cleaner, follow the maker's instructions. It will be the most satisfactory method.

Furniture next. Any bad marks, such as scent stains, will have to be dealt with in advance, but give any pieces that look a bit smeary a soap-and-water treatment. As with the carpet, have two bowls of water, one soapy, one for rinsing. Have cloths very well wrung out, so that they are damp rather than wet. Dry each portion as you go along. In a home without children, where the furniture gets regular intelligent care, the washing won't be necessary. But if there are marks, or, in your enthusiasm, you have been a bit heavy-handed with the polish, washing is a wonderful reviver. When quite dry, but not before, apply a very little furniture cream or polish and rub up well. The polishing can, in fact, well be left until another occasion; you have already accomplished a lot of work.

Before you call it a day, replace furniture and ornaments, re-hang pictures and mirrors, make up the bed and put up fresh curtains. You can sleep well tonight, knowing that even the Victorian housewife wouldn't have done a more thorough job.

THE METHOD FOR THE SITTING-ROOM.

Spring-cleaning the sitting-room proceeds on much the same lines, only here there are cabinets, cupboards or bookshelves to turn out instead of wardrobes and chests of drawers. There will probably be more ornaments and pictures, too. As with the bedroom, treat the interiors of furniture, with contents, as a separate job to be done ahead, and in instalments if need be.

Electric-light fittings can also be looked to before the general clean. Frayed wires need making good. Bulbs benefit from a wipe with a damp cloth, while shades need something more than the routine brush. A dry-clean with a grease solvent, or a damp sponge with soapy water, according to material and condition, will make all the difference to their appearance.

Having got as many preliminaries out of the way as possible, the order on the appointed day should be approximately as follows:

First, collect all loose ornaments, china, pictures, mirrors and so forth, and take them to the kitchen for washing or appropriate treatment.

Second, take down curtains and take up loose rugs. If these are to be suction cleaned, do it straight away before removing from the room.

Third, move furniture, either out of the room, or to the middle, away from the walls, as far as possible. Cover up.

Fourth, brush down ceilings and walls and do any sponging over or dry cleaning necessary.

Fifth, deal with the upholstered furniture. In addition to the regular brushing or going over with the vacuum-cleaner attachment, the coverings, unless you have loose covers, will benefit from a rather more thorough treatment. If only slightly soiled, sponging with grease solvent will probably do the trick. Otherwise, a shampoo, similar to that recommended for carpets, should be given. Either use one of the new branded soapless cleaners, advertised as specially good for this kind of work, or make up your own solution. Half soap flakes and half liquid soap substitute, in the proportions of a table-spoonful of each to half a pint of hot water, is good. Work as when cleaning the carpet, being sure to rinse with clear water, and to take care that each portion dealt with overlaps the last. Never have your cloth or brush more than damp; it's not wise to get upholstery wet. Dry as much as possible with an absorbent cloth.

Furniture upholstered in hide will naturally want a different treatment. To a pint of cold water add a dessertspoonful of vinegar and half a teaspoonful of the strong liquid ammonia. Sponge all over with this. Mop dry and rub in a little castor oil. Leave to dry and finish off by an application of colorless shoe cream and a good rub with a soft cloth.

Sixth, tackle the paintwork.

Seventh, give the floors an extra good clean. If these are of parquet or light oak blocks, they may show marks or discoloration. *Don't* scrub, but rub the way of the grain with medium steel wool. If the condition is very bad, dip the wool in 'turps' substitute. This job is hard on the hands, so wear old leather gloves.

Eighth, deal with polished furniture. If marked or smeary, wash as described on p. 81. When quite dry, apply a very little polish, and after leaving for a while, rub up well. Very resistant stains on natural wood, waxed oak or pine can be sandpapered. Afterwards, apply a little colourless wax polish as usual. Replace ornaments and pictures, hang fresh curtains, put on loose covers, if you have them, and complete the finishing touches.

THE KITCHEN AND BATHROOM.

Excess steam is usually the main problem in kitchen and bathroom. Try to have walls and ceilings repainted with washable paint, unless of course they are tiled, just as often as they seem to want it. If actual repainting is not practicable or necessary, a complete wash down of the walls with hot water and a little sugar soap or paste cleaner is a wise measure.

When doing the kitchen, don't forget the inside of the larder. It needs to be specially fresh and clean, so be generous with the washable paint. The rest of the kitchen cleaning will merely be an elaboration of the weekly routine, with all the things that have been left undone throughout the year made good in one glorious orgy of cleanliness. If, in spite of a good scrub, the hard-used linoleum-covered floor still shows an occasional black mark, rub gently with steel wool. Polish up in the normal way.

GUARD AGAINST MOTHS.

Anti-moth treatment takes up the time, but is part of the spring-cleaning ritual that should never be neglected, even if it has to be deferred until after the general cleaning has been done. Bear in mind that the moth's greatest ally is dirt or dust of any kind. Don't be misled by the fact that your husband's dress suit, say, looks in perfect condition, or that he never really wore his town overcoat, but preferred his old 'British warm'. Choose a nice sunny day and have everything out.

Brush all winter clothes carefully, being specially scrupulous with masculine attire. Trouser turn-ups, and behind collars and inside pockets tend to collect all kinds of fluff and grit, and so have a great attraction for moths. So go over these parts with minute attention. If there are any general soil marks, send for dry-cleaning. If this is not necessary, go round collars with a grease solvent. This done, leave the clothes in the sun out of doors for airing. Before replacing in the newly scrubbed wardrobe, attach a little bag, made of butter muslin or a length of old silk stocking, to each coat hanger. In it put a tablespoonful of paradichlorbenzene crystals. These are obtainable at most chemists and a pound goes quite a long way.

Even after all this, don't rest on your laurels. Go through your wardrobe, *and have everything out* for a check up every month or so. It's the only safe way.

Fur coats should be brushed and cleaned similarly, if not sent for professional cleaning and storage. Either hang in the wardrobe in a special cover, with plenty of paradichlorbenzene, or pack away in a sealed container. To make these yourself, simply use strong brown paper and seal the edges with adhesive tape or paper strips. Don't forget your anti-moth crystals inside, and don't leave too long without attention.

Knitted jumpers and sweaters should be washed before packing away. If left in a drawer, look over during the summer to see whether the crystals have evaporated and need replenishing. Do this with woollen underwear, too. In a centrally-heated house or flat it's wise to go through wardrobes or chests every few weeks right through the year; moths seem to revel in the comfortable warmth.

HOW TO REMOVE MARKS AND STAINS.

Although they won't necessarily be done at spring-cleaning time, there are one or two refurbishing jobs that don't come into the ordinary weekly routine.

Heat Marks on Furniture.

For instance, removing heat marks from polished furniture. This is a little tricky, and is only likely to succeed if the damage is not too great. However, if after a dinner-party you see an unwelcome ring, it's worth trying. Make a pad of cotton wool and pour on one or two drops of methylated spirit. Cover with two thicknesses of butter muslin and rub over and around the marks, using a circular motion. The object is to remove just sufficient stain from the surrounding undamaged part of the wood to mask the discoloration. Later, polish as usual.

Scent Marks and Water Stains on Polished Wood.

Water stains left by flower vases, rings from glasses, and scent marks will often respond to the same treatment. If much harm has been done, professional repolishing is the only remedy. Incidentally, it's a good plan to have covered with plate glass occasional tables on which glasses are liable to be put down.

Ink on Carpets or Upholstery.

Ink on carpets is another small casualty liable to occur at any time. If spilt freshly, wipe up as much as possible with a damp cloth or blotting paper. Then get to work to remove the stain. Oxalic acid, a useful, though poisonous, chemical, is simplest. Make a hot solution, in the proportion of a teaspoonful of crystals to a half pint of water. Apply a teaspoonful or so and leave for a moment. Then wipe away with a cloth damped with fresh water. Two or three applications may be necessary, with a careful rinsing after each. (Oxalic acid is now difficult to obtain.)

An alternative method is the permanganate of potash and hydrogen peroxide one. Make a solution of the former at a strength of half a teaspoonful of crystals to just under a pint of water, and dilute the peroxide (10 vol.) with three parts of water. First dab on the permanganate solution. This will take the ink out but leave a brown stain. Rinse with a damp cloth and apply the peroxide. Leave on for a second or two and then rinse off. Again you may have to repeat the treatment several times.

Tarnish Marks on Brass or Copper.

Oxalic acid will also work wonders with very badly tarnished brass or copper. Use a rather stronger solution than for the ink, say a teaspoonful to a third of a pint of water, and rub over the neglected metal with an old cloth. Rinse straight away. Finally wash in soapy water and dry thoroughly. Afterwards polish in the ordinary way. For the sake of your hands, wear gloves when using oxalic acid as it is very corrosive.

Soot Marks on Carpets.

It's a careful sweep that doesn't leave a trace of soot behind on the carpet, but it's not too serious. Get up what you can and then apply a grease solvent to the marks.

Chapter X

HOW TO LOOK AFTER EQUIPMENT

"OH, WILL you have a look at the vacuum cleaner, dear? It won't work!" How often does that cry greet a returning husband! Not that it's a bad idea to get the man of the house to do any mechanical repairs needed as part of his contribution to home-making. But all the same, there's no doubt that many a suction cleaner, and many an iron or lamp too, just 'blows' because of carelessness in use, or insufficient checking over. *Never* pull on the flex to remove an electric plug from the socket; handle the plug itself. Get into the habit of looking over the connection every time you put the particular appliance away after use. If you see that the flex is beginning to pull out or fray, get the repair done before it is forgotten about.

If you have to handle such jobs yourself, here's the way to set about it.

HOW TO REPAIR A FLEX.

First of all, a word as to the why and wherefore. Electricity flows through wire in exactly the same way as water flows through a pipe. If the pipe is burst, you know perfectly well that water will not run from the tap. Just so with electricity. Any break or faulty connection from the source of supply to the appliance will result in stoppage or darkness. Damage to wires usually occurs at the plug. Remove plug from socket and open up plug by unscrewing bolts holding the two halves or cover plate. Remove ends of wires from plug after carefully noting the colours of the rubber coverings fixed to each pin, whether two or three, and also the way in which the ends of the wire are secured to the pins. Cut flex some three inches from end, thereby shortening the flex by that amount. Then remove the outer covering from two inches of the cut end of the flex. This will expose two or three rubber-covered wires. Bind the outer covering with some thirty turns of thread or cotton to prevent unravelling and strip half an inch of rubber covering from the ends of the wires. Attach ends of wires to pins in exactly the same order and method as they were before removal. Make sure everything is tight, and that no exposed wire is visible. Replace cover of plug.

CARE OF THE VACUUM CLEANER.

Apart from seeing that the flex is correctly connected to the plug, little more than common sense is needed to keep the vacuum cleaner running sweetly. Don't give it the strain of picking up pins or other hard objects, which may cut or nick the belt, and don't neglect the emptying after use recommended by the makers. If dirt is left in the bag, the suction can't be quite so powerful and, therefore, efficient. Emptying is sometimes put off as it is rather a dusty job. Try using a carrier bag, instead of a sheet of newspaper. The vacuum bag can be emptied straight into the former, and dirt won't fly about. Incidentally, in your enthusiasm for cleanliness, don't wash the bag. Cleaning with a whisk brush is the correct way.

Every so often, examine the cleaner a little more closely. Brushes get worn after a while and need adjusting or replacing. Always keep brushes clean. Hair should be removed often. A slack belt will destroy efficiency, so look that over every six months, say, too. Finally, follow the maker's instructions as to lubrication and general care. Haphazard oiling will do more harm than good, but careful lubrication according to instructions does help.

Daily emptying is the rule with the faithful carpet sweeper too, *and* attention to brushes. These slip out of their sockets quite easily and are all the better for keeping free of the hairs and cottons that tend to get wrapped tightly round them. Again, follow the maker's instructions as regards oiling.

MOPS AND BRUSHES.

Mops should be hung by the handles, not rested on their head. Apart from this, cleanliness is the only rule. Shake freely after use, and every so often give them a shampoo in a pail. After wash-day is the time for this, when there is some nice soapy water left over. Rinse well and hang, or reverse, out of doors to dry.

Brushes need similar care; and do remember that it's always easier to wash lightly, rather than badly soiled articles. So get into the habit of checking over brushes and mops just as you do your dusters. Wash these out every day if possible. Save soap ends, keep them in a soap-saver and whisk up a lather when the daily sweeping and dusting is done. It takes a few minutes only, and gets your hands clean too, so it's worth the little effort.

Floor-polisher brushes should be dry-cleaned with grease

solvent, *not* washed. Hair brushes are best left in strong ammonia water for a little while. Take care that the backs are not submerged. Then agitate for a moment and they will be free of dust and dirt. Very greasy masculine brushes may need two waters, but there's no need for soap. Rinse first in hot, then in cold water and dry, if possible, in a current of air.

BOILER.

How to clean cooking stoves was dealt with in Chapter VIII, p. 71. Regular care, and the correct fuel, is also the secret of solid-fuel hot-water boilers. Each type of stove has its own idiosyncrasies, but with systematic riddling, periodic cleaning out and intelligent following of the instructions, nothing much should go wrong.

WASHING MACHINES.

With the fully automatic washing machine, all you have to do is to follow the book. Cleaning out sometimes presents difficulties with the simpler kinds, and also with wash-boilers. The secret of removing that nasty scum ring, caused by hard water, is to deal with it while still warm. Rub over with scouring powder *immediately* after use.

REFRIGERATORS.

Keep moist food, such as salads, meat, fish, milk and puddings, in the special containers, or otherwise covered. Never put warm food in the cabinet. Allow to cool off first. Never leave the door even ajar, and defrost regularly, according to the instructions supplied by the makers.

Chapter XI

FEEDING THE FAMILY

KEEPING a home clean and bright is certainly necessary, but seeing that the family gets appetising and nourishing meals is the very essence of the housewife's job. In some ways it has never been harder; in others it's much simplified from the days of plenty. Gradually we have all grown to be less exacting in our demands. A meal that would be greeted with the warmest approval to-day would have been thought very ordinary before the war. There are less materials on which to lavish culinary skill, and so less demands on the cook. So what we lose on the roundabouts of shopping difficulties we're likely to pick up on the swings of not having the wherewithal for, say, extensive cake making.

All the same, shopping and cooking together take up a sizeable part of the working day, probably anything from a third to a half. So as in all other departments of homemaking, a well-thought-out plan pays every time.

CHOOSE SHOPS CAREFULLY.

Planning the shopping begins with choosing the shops at which you will deal. If they are conveniently grouped together, time will be saved. On the other hand, it may work out better to go a little farther afield if by so doing queueing and waiting time can be cut out. Then there's the question of method in the shops themselves. If at the grocer's you have to go to four distinct counters—one for bacon, one for fats, one for dry-goods and another for cleaning materials—as happens at some stores, the time spent on the weekly order is likely to be double, or even more, than that necessary when one assistant 'serves through'.

The question of whether the grocer chosen carries the brands you prefer, and has a normally well-assorted stock, is another point to weigh up before registering. If not, and time has to be spent on 'shop crawling' to get necessary 'points' goods, say, that are available in the district but not with your supplier, you will have made a bad bargain in your choice.

Then what about deliveries? If you live far from a shopping centre, or for any reason are handicapped from getting out and about, you may have to choose those retailers who will take your order at the door and later deliver the goods. Otherwise, you will probably find that shopping in person enables you to do rather better. So many goods are in short supply that it's a question of being on the spot when they come in. Also, shopping is an excellent way of getting you out into the air. Too many housewives, unless they have young children who must have a daily constitutional, tend to get housebound.

DON'T QUEUE UNNECESSARILY.

But, once more, common sense must be your guide. The woman who spends her time flitting from shop to shop, standing in queues almost for the sake of it, is no good manager. In fact, she is the one who wails longest about the difficulties of getting food and the hardship of her lot generally. It is her family who often have to put up with the sketchiest meals; for so long has been spent on the hunt that there is no time left for the preparation of the spoils. In any contest for home-makers we'd mark her lowest!

So, before you decide on where you will give your custom, explore your district carefully, make some casual purchases, hear what neighbours have to say about the various facilities. Then balance the pros and cons, and finally decide. Once you've registered, be a cheerful shopper! You'll fare much better, and find that, with its human contacts, shopping is a pleasant interlude in the daily round, not the dreary chore some people make it.

A SHOPPING ROUTINE PAYS.

Butcher, baker, grocer, greengrocer, fishmonger, dairy; how often should it be necessary to visit each? If you pay the milkman, you may never need to go to the dairy, while with the baker calling it will only be necessary to shop for the occasional cake. Nowadays, once, or twice at most, a week is usual for the butcher's. Twice weekly for the grocer's is probably a good idea, too. With a once-a-week call the chances are that some goods in short supply will be missed. Going more often tends to waste both your time and the shop assistant's, so does not pay in the long run. How often the greengrocer is visited will be determined by the distance from the shops. If it's only a short walk, the fresher the vegetables the better. Or you may be fortunate in having a travelling greengrocer who will call on you several days weekly. Whether you have set days for fish, or decide when you see what the fishmonger's slabs look like, will also depend on how often you can visit the shop.

So plan your shopping routine, and stick to it as far as possible. If the grocer knows you come with your main order on Tuesday, say, there's a good chance that anything special coming in the day before may be saved for you. Similarly, if the butcher expects a call on Wednesday for sausages, or the occasional offal, you will be taken into account when he does the allocation. You'll soon get to know whether the greengrocer has the weekend stocks in on Friday afternoon, or whether it's wiser to wait until Saturday morning. The latter is a busy time with the shops, so if you can do most of your buying ahead there will be less waiting.

BUDGET 'POINTS'.

Thus far we've considered shopping merely from the point of view of time spent. This is important, since the single-handed housewife must use her energies to best advantage, but it touches only the fringe of the problem. The real test comes at the table. Are the meals served as good and appetising as possible under present conditions? Most home-makers have always had the task of spending the housekeeping allowance to the best advantage. Now there is the allied one of getting the best return for 'points' and non-rationed goods in terms of nourishment, too.

Every month, when any 'points' changes have been announced, make up a rough budget. It's not sufficient to spend 'points' to buy just what you fancy. They must be used to supplement basic rations, so that balanced meals, providing the nutritional essentials, can be served up each day.

A BRIEF GUIDE TO NUTRITIONAL VALUES.

As a start, you must have a clear idea of the nutritional job done by various foods.

PROTEINS.

Meat and poultry of all kinds, including offal, also fish, eggs, cheese and milk, are protein foods. So are, to a much lesser degree, 'pulses', that is, peas, lentils, haricot beans and also soya. Protein foods are builders. That is why they are so essential to children and adolescents when rapid growth is being made. Right through our life we need these foods to maintain strength, both physical and mental. Without them, concentration and ability to do work of any kind would deteriorate rapidly. From the practical angle, then, the housewife must see that a 'builder' food is served at every main meal, and more often if possible. On meatless days, cheese or fish must be substituted, with perhaps eggs at another meal. If the helping of meat is on the small side, dried peas served as a third vegetable will help restore the balance, and so on.

CARBOHYDRATES, FATS AND SUGAR.

Bread, potatoes and cereals come into the carbohydrates group; that is, the starchy foods whose main job is as 'fillers'. Together with fats and sugars they give warmth and a certain amount of energy. In cold weather the body craves for them, but taken too generously they result in over-heaviness and sluggishness. 'Fillers' are very necessary, of course, especially when much physical work is done, but it's a bad diet that depends too much on them.

The rest of our food needs are supplied by the various vitamins and minerals. Many foodstuffs are composites, containing either protein or carbohydrates with one or more vitamins or minerals. Foremost among these is milk, which as well as being valuable protein is rich in vitamins A and D and calcium, and also contains iodine.

VITAMINS A AND D.

Oily fish such as herrings, and cod liver and halibut liver, are splendid sources of these same vitamins as well as having good protein value. Vitamins A and D, sometimes known as the 'sunshine vitamins' because they are necessary to vitality and sense of well-being, and also for their value in reinforcing the body against infections, are also found in butter, vitaminised margarine, cod liver oil and, to a lesser degree, in eggs.

VITAMINS B_1 AND B_2.

Without vitamins B_1 and B_2, you can't feel well, and may suffer from all kinds of 'deficiency' complaints. They come in the embryo of wheat and in yeast products. National bread, which is coarsely milled to retain as much as possible of this wheat germ, is therefore a good protective, as well as an energy-giving food. White bread, from which the best part of the wheat has been refined away, is not nearly so good for us. When we could get plenty of other protein foods, such as meat, which contains this vitamin, it didn't matter if our bread had little food value. Now it's of vital importance.

VITAMIN C.

Fresh fruit and green vegetables supply the all-important vitamin C. Lack of it is the cause of a good deal of vague ill-health. Spongy gums, a low resistance to infection and colds, decaying teeth, as well as excessive tiredness, dullness and a general muddy look, may all be traced to not having enough green vegetables of the right kind. For all fruits and 'greens' are not equally rich in vitamin C. While a serving of black currants will contribute nearly all the C vitamins necessary for health each day, rhubarb gives very few. Similarly, purple-sprouting broccoli is almost twice as rich in vitamin C as cauliflower or cabbage. Onions come very low on the list. All the citrous fruits are brimful of vitamin C, so when they are plentiful it pays to serve them as much as possible.

Although the amount of vitamin C varies according to the variety of fruit and vegetables, there is always much more when food is fresh. Stale 'greens' are almost useless from the vitamin point of view, so are over-cooked ones. The golden rule is: shop for the freshest, prepare at the last minute, and cook quickly in as little water as possible.

So, knowing that the meat and bacon ration plus the egg allowance and the little bit of cheese doesn't give us as much protein value as is desirable, you will see that the menu is supplemented with fish, fresh or canned, and additional 'points' cheese or dried eggs. In winter, 'points' used for dried peas, haricot beans or lentils are well spent. They add bulk and warmth to meals, and also have some protein value, too.

Biscuits are very agreeable and make a pleasant snack, but they take a lot of 'points'. From the nutriment angle they must be looked on as a luxury, only to be indulged in occasionally. On the other hand, canned citrous juices are better than most tonics that come from a bottle. Dried fruits are the making of cakes and puddings, but they're also a useful source of iron and calcium as well as sugar. Milk, evaporated or condensed, makes it easier to liven up the menu, and it's also a wonderful protective food. Syrup helps in cooking if you've a sweet tooth, but though extra sugar is pleasant, it's not something we really *need*. Before the war, many of us had too much of it for good health.

PLAN MENUS AHEAD.

'Points' budgeting having been done roughly for the month, for uncertainty of supplies makes it impossible to be too exact, the next job is to get down to menu-planning. This is best done on a weekly basis though, even so, a certain amount of flexibility is necessary.

On Monday morning, or better still on Sunday night after supper, go through the larder and check up on remainders. Have a look at the store-cupboard, too. It's a good plan to keep a permanent list of all commodities in stock. Put a mark against anything that is running low and then it will take only a minute or two to make out your lists on the day you go to the grocer's. Then, after reviewing what is on hand, and bearing in mind what is likely to be obtainable, jot down an outline of the proposed meals until the next weekend.

Monday's main meal will probably be worked out around the remains of the joint, whether served cold or made-up in some form or another.

For Tuesday there may still be a little meat to use with, say, spaghetti. Alternatively, the main course will have to be fish.

On Wednesday, sausages in some form or another will appear, unless it's the offal week, or part of the meat ration is taken.

Thursday you will have to contrive a meal of some kind, perhaps half of the previous day's sausages made into a pie, or a vegetable and cheese or egg main dish. Fish will be 'on' again for Friday.

Shortcomings in the main course must be made good with an extra nourishing pudding, or some soup first of all. If the meal looks like being filling and appetising, but rather low in vitamin C, a glass of fruit or tomato juice as an appetiser will put that right. You'll have to eke out materials in short supply. If you served up a fruit pie for the weekend, the fat situation will probably not allow such indulgence until the next week. You may be able to spare 'points' suet for a boiled fruit pudding, if the weather is cold, or serve a sweet batter, with or without fruit, when eggs are plentiful. Milk puddings won't present much difficulty during early summer, but for the rest of the year alternatives will have to be found fairly often, unless 'points' are allotted for extra canned milk. If a good deal of stewed fruit is being used, sugar will become a problem, which will mean either a heavier purchase of syrup or the part substitution of saccharine for sugar, especially in tea or coffee.

A tip to make the rationed goods last out as well as possible, and also to keep the household expenditure on an even keel, is to portion out purchases over the month. Take the sugar ration for the month on half the books one week, and the rest in a fortnight's time. Divide up the tea and soap flakes buying similarly, also cleaning materials and 'extras'. With 'points' goods, it is probably wiser to get them when available, or else it may be a case of being left with nothing.

One advantage of planning meals a week at a time is that you see how your stores will work out and can spot in time if you are likely to run dangerously short of anything. Also, it's often possible to 'work in' the cooking of two meals together, as will be shown in the next chapter.

Of course, it's fatal to stick too hard and fast to your plans; they should be merely a guide. If you are able to get a rabbit, for instance, or there is a glut of a special kind of fish, or cauliflowers just right for a special *au gratin* dish and a good 'buy', a last-minute switch around is only common sense.

Chapter XII

METHOD IN THE KITCHEN

"CLEAR up as you go, that's the secret," said a male 'expert' loftily. That's sound enough, but it's only a very small part of the picture, as the gentleman in question would soon have discovered if his culinary experience had been of the day-to-day variety, not just the occasional preparation of a special dish or meal.

To get through the rather monotonous cookery round demanded of to-day's housewife with some enjoyment as well as efficiency, calls for two essentials. The first is a conveniently planned 'workshop', with all the tools so placed that unnecessary work and steps are eliminated.

GOOD COOKING EQUIPMENT SAVES WORK.

As we said in Chapter III when discussing the tools for the job, do be sure to have the right kind of equipment. A pair of sharp scissors, preferably stainless, will halve the time needed in rinding bacon, taking fins and tails off fish, cutting up certain kinds of meat, and many other jobs, too. Of course, you'll have to guard these like a dragon! Otherwise they'll be borrowed for all kinds of unsuitable jobs, and never be in their place. From the start, train the family to regard these kitchen scissors as *sacred.*

The correct kind of knife also makes a lot of difference. Chopping with a cook's knife, which has a blade deeper than the handle and so leaves room for the fingers to hold the latter without their being rapped on the board all the time, is less fatiguing than if an ordinary table-knife is used. The same knife, if kept sharp, is good for filleting. A long slender round-tipped one, also kept sharp, cuts cooked meat into really thin slices; while you *must* have a nice short-bladed vegetable-knife to get on with any speed. Add to your list a flexible palette-knife for scraping the mixing-bowl, turning things in the frying-pan and many other uses besides, and a saw-edged knife for bread cutting. Whatever you do, don't forget the humble potato-peeler. It's worth many times its price. All these are not fancy extras, but the right tools for their respective jobs.

The same applies to strainers, sieves, egg-whisks, graters, measuring cups and spoons, also scales, a mincing machine, and sufficient bowls and cooking pots of various sizes and types to avoid perpetual washing-up while food preparation is in hand. They can be done without, but it makes the work more awkward and heavy. Nothing suggested in the list given in Chapter III, p. 25, is an extravagance.

In choosing saucepans, especially, do be ruled by quality rather than price. Aluminium pans of good quality and finish, which doesn't necessarily mean a highly polished one, will easily last twenty years or more, with reasonable care. "If only I'd known how good saucepans can lighten the work and save worry about the results, I'd have gone without anything almost to have them," said a housewife, now in much better circumstances than when she married soon after the first world war. For years she bought and discarded cheap pans, thinking she was being thrifty. A year or so ago she refitted her kitchen with well-chosen saucepans, casseroles and so on. She says the difference can only be appreciated by one who has suffered from using inferior tools. "I tell my daughter to furnish the kitchen first and leave the lounge till later, if need be; she'll make her husband happier."

Generally speaking, fairly heavy (though not ground-based) pans are best with all types of stoves, not only for the electric and solid-fuel heat-storage ones, for which they are essential. For these last, ground-based ones are recommended. Heavy pans take a little longer to heat up, which may seem a disadvantage on gas or oil cookers, but they don't burn nearly so easily, last incomparably longer, and retain their heat much better, thus minimising the risk of food cooling while waiting to be dished up.

Four saucepans of various sizes is the minimum that can be considered satisfactory, even for a family of two, and half a dozen is not too many. Some, if not all, should be of the type that can be used interchangeably in the oven or on the hot-plate. If good-quality pans are chosen, and they are kept shining, they can go to the serving table just as well as fireproof china or glass, thus cutting out work. A double saucepan is scarcely a necessity, but it is very useful. A steamer, on the other hand, is really a 'must', though one improvised with an adaptable colander-type top that will fit on several pans will answer almost as well as those sold complete in three tiers.

Do have a separate frying-pan for fish. A curved-sided omelette-pan, that can be reserved for omelettes and pancakes, is a pleasant extra. Two grill-pans can't be considered an extravagance, for one used for herrings or similar strong-smelling fish will soon tend to smell, in spite of careful washing.

Pressure cookers, or more exactly pressure saucepans, for the multi-purpose cooker has been in use for a number of years, are a comparatively recent addition to the battery of cooking pots. Their initial outlay is high, but in some households they undoubtedly pay. They are perhaps particularly useful for the home-maker who has an outside job and so has to get meals in a rush. Handled properly, they do conserve the goodness of various foodstuffs. At this stage, they can scarcely be called essential equipment, but it's a good idea to see various types demonstrated and decide whether they would be a sound investment in one's particular circumstances.

LEARN TO LOOK AHEAD.

Just as important as the right tools is the kind of mind that thinks ahead and, wherever possible, works in two jobs at once. Above all, one thing has to be guarded against. Don't let kitchen duty drag on throughout the day. Far better a short, sharp bout of concentrated effort.

Whenever you start to cook, see that everything you will have to use is placed to hand. This applies to both ingredients and tools. As you finish with an ingredient, pop it away in larder or store-cupboard. Whenever a saucepan comes off the stove or a dish is finished with, put it to soak in the sink. Then, when you come to wash-up, as soon as your cooking is finished, the work will be half done.

The kitchen time-table will largely depend on whether the main meal is taken at midday or in the evening. In the latter case, cooking time will be mainly after tea, though dishes that want a long, slow cooking must be put on ahead. Try to work two days' cooking in one as much as possible. To do this successfully, you must think ahead when marketing, which is where the value of menu-planning comes in.

'WORK IN' TWO MEALS TOGETHER.

Supposing your joint is best and middle end of neck of lamb or mutton. This is quite a good 'buy', as the middle neck is cheaper and therefore the joint is not so pathetically small as if all 'best end' were chosen.

Roast the best cutlets with potatoes and braised onions, or make onion sauce if you have time, and make a hot-pot of the rest. Potatoes and onions for both dishes can be prepared together, and both go into the oven at the same time. On the second day, when the hot-pot is served, it will only need to be put into the oven, with the lid off, long enough for the potatoes to brown on top. Breast of mutton, which will provide two days' dinner for two people on one ration book, can be treated similarly.

When there are children, and a midday dinner is necessary, the morning must be kitchen-time. Cake making and extra jobs will sometimes have to be left until the afternoon, but in this case, make them the special task for the day, instead of doing any of the weekly cleaning. There will probably be the added complication that your husband will want his dinner at night. To avoid having too much on hand then, try to do most of the preparation with the midday meal.

For instance, if the midday main dish is shepherd's pie, make a separate individual-portion dish for the evening. Partially cook it with the rest, taking care that it is not browned too much, or allowed to get dry. Then in the evening it can be heated through and appetisingly crisped up, either in the oven or under the grill. It won't take a few minutes to cook fresh greens, but wash them in the morning and keep in a covered saucepan. If they have to be shredded, as with cabbage, do this just before cooking. The soup for your own and the children's meal can be made ahead; your husband will most likely enjoy a bowlful, too. With room to spare in the oven during the morning, baked custards and fruit for the children's supper can go in, allowing enough for two meals. If the weather were cold, the midday pudding might be baked suet-roll. You would make an extra one, covered carefully with greaseproof paper to avoid it getting baked up and hard, for the evening.

Next day, with more housework to do, cooking must be as simple as possible, so choose a steamed meal. Use the bottom of the steamer for a light sponge pudding or batter. The next compartment will take potatoes, and on the top, fillets of fish between two plates. The only extra, some parsley sauce, can be made just before dishing up. A glass of fruit or tomato juice as a first course can take the place of a green vegetable.

If steamed fish is not popular with the returning breadwinner, give him a grilled fillet with a little parsley butter. While it is cooking, slice up the steamed potatoes left over for the purpose and sauté them in a pan on top of the grill. With the fruit and custard to follow, or some steamed pudding if preferred, there is an appetising, well-balanced meal without much extra work.

HAVE OVEN DAYS . . .

When the oven is on you want to use it to the uttermost. Stewed fruit, baked custard, milk puddings of various kinds, baked batters and suet puddings, pastry and sponge puddings, give a big choice. Don't forget savouries, too, either as a second course instead of a sweet, or for the main dish the following day. Alternatively, cakes can be baked when roasting or casserole cooking occupies part, but not all, of the oven space.

While on the subject of the oven, remember that care in its use can minimise oven cleaning quite a lot. Meat roasted at a low temperature rather than the high one that used to be considered correct, shrinks less, is just as tender, and soils the oven less, too. Alternatively, use a Dutch-oven type of tin, with lid. It saves splashes and keeps in the juices of the meat. Remove the lid to brown the potatoes. If surplus fat is poured off then, and the oven turned high, the potatoes will be crisp, and the meat too, but the oven won't get encrusted with fat. Take care that fruit tarts and milk puddings don't boil over. With the former, cook some of the fruit separately and keep that in the pie-dish on the dry side. Never have a hot oven for the puddings. *Always* wipe over the oven with a damp cloth while still hot. Marks come off much more easily then.

There is one exception, apart from the occasional sauce, to the rule of 'It's an oven day, cook everything in it', and that is green vegetables. Thanks to the Ministry of Food advertisements, even the beginner knows they need to be quickly cooked, and prepared only just before being plunged into the fast-boiling water. However, they take so little time and fuel to cook that it can't be considered extravagant to use the top of the stove for them alone.

. . . AND TOP-OF-THE-STOVE ONES.

Do group together top-of-the-stove dishes in the same way as oven-cooked ones. Stew, say, can well be accompanied by a steamed pudding or pancakes, unless something has already been cooked in advance. Two or more things can be cooked over one flame, when steaming, either with a regular or an improvised steamer, is the method used. In addition to potatoes, fish, for fish cakes to be eaten at breakfast next day, could be cooked, together with a steamed pudding. Or fish cooked like this could be served creamed with a good sauce for the following evening.

When you want to have a 'light' cooking day, try preparing something such as spaghetti on the previous one. If you are already tied to the kitchen, superintending the stew and accompaniments, the extra work is not much trouble. While the spaghetti cooks, you make the sauce, then place layers of spaghetti, sauce and grated cheese in a fireproof dish. Next day, it's only a question of heating through in the oven or under the grill and cooking a green vegetable, and there's your main course.

If you get into the habit of thinking and working on these lines, you should find that the enjoyment of doing a creative job intelligently and well outweighs the physical work involved. It's only when cooking is allowed to deteriorate into an unimaginative chore, or there is an overwhelming amount of it to be got through, that it becomes hard or disagreeable work.

STOCK THE STORE CUPBOARD INTELLIGENTLY.

One thing more that will help in the easy preparation of meals is having a certain amount of ready-cooked, or ready-to-use food in the store-cupboard. Dehydrated vegetables, for instance, especially onions, are a boon for stews, soups or sauces. Good bouillon, tomato or meat-extract cubes are helpful for the same things. Bottled tomatoes and canned tomato juice save time and trouble.

Such things as baked beans and salmon can prove of value in an emergency, but as the latter is so expensive in 'points' it shouldn't be used too often. There are, however, a number of 'points free' canned goods, of which full use should be made. Cod's roe, a newcomer to the market, can be served as it is, cold, with salad or in sandwiches, or it makes a delicious hot dish cut in slices and fried. Canned herrings, in oil or tomato, are also good cold or hot. Then there are the canned pâtés which can be spun out in jellied moulds or similar summer dishes. A few tins of corned beef, which may sometimes be taken instead of the fresh-meat ration, are a wonderful standby. One small tin makes four good servings if not dressed up in any way, and a good many more if used in a composite dish.

The ready-cooked steam puddings are helpful, while some cooks like packet mixtures for puddings and cakes.

Generally speaking, they don't contain much beyond flour (with or without a small percentage of cornflour, ryeflour or soya), with a raising agent, colouring and flavouring, but they can be useful in an emergency if a tested brand is used. Flavoured jellies come on 'points', so on the whole the various brands of gelatine are preferable, though again the former will save some time on occasion.

Coming more into the luxury class, but well worth while if the budget will run to them, are tins of dressed-crab-meat paste, shrimps, oysters and clams. All are good for patties, when a little goes a long way, or for giving a rather special touch to sauces. Gherkins, olives and several kinds of pickles and chutney also help to put zest into fairly plain dishes, without much trouble. It's worth keeping a good stock of fresh herbs, and also paprika, curry powder, tobasco and any other flavourings you like, as well as several different kinds of sauces, ready-made salad-dressing, oil and vinegar.

With some kinds of ready-prepared foodstuffs you must do the initial work yourself. You'll soon discover what a saving of time there is if you have grated cheese or suet at hand. They both keep quite well in a jar with a transparent jam cover. Ready-cleaned dried fruit, too, will help you to whip up a cake or a pudding in a hurry. How to make time for 'extra' cooking, we'll see in the next chapter.

Chapter XIII

FITTING IN THE 'EXTRA' COOKING JOBS

"I DON'T know how you do it," says a young bride to an older, long-married friend. "Your house always looks spotless, you are a wonderful cook, there's always cake and home-made jam on the tea-table, and you even bottle your own fruit and make chutney, yet you manage to find time for all kinds of outside interests, too. The days are never long enough for me, and yet I don't get through as much." To which the older woman's reply is: "Experience counts, my dear."

With every phase of house-running this is certainly true, but never more so than with cooking. At first you scarcely dare do anything without the cookery book at your elbow. Ingredients are scrupulously weighed out, you suffer agonies of uncertainty wondering whether your cake mixture is wet enough, your fats sufficiently rubbed in or creamed enough, or whether the moment has come to add the sugar to the preserves-pan full of boiling fruit. Lack of manual dexterity makes you slow, so does your nervousness as to whether you are proceeding on the right lines. At this stage in one's culinary career, making a cake or a batch of pastry is an exhausting experience.

Later on, you get more sure of yourself, and begin to speed up in your work. You still need your cookery book, or books, but you know that every word needn't be taken literally. Cooking is an important business, agreed, but one of the first things the woman at home has to learn is to divide her energies, so that she can manage two or three jobs more or less at once! So don't break your heart when you can't 'follow the book' in every detail. You learn that quite a lot of latitude is possible, that even small mistakes won't necessarily result in spoiled eatables. When this stage of assurance has been reached, it's time to sit back and review your methods dispassionately and see whether improvements can be made.

If there's not a great deal of housework, and especially in a family of two, it may be perfectly practicable for the home-maker to have a baking afternoon once or twice a week. It's pleasant to experiment with various attractive recipes. When children come, or other added responsibilities, there's often just not the time. If cakes are to be made at all, they must, more often than not, be worked in with the general routine.

HAVE A REPERTOIRE OF TESTED RECIPES.

The most successful way of doing this is to have a small repertoire of selected recipes that are so familiar they can be made up almost automatically. With such recipes, there is no need to get out the scales. So many cupfuls of flour, a lump of fat so big, a handful of dried fruits, so many drops of flavouring—you get to know exactly what is required. If something is missing from the store-cupboard your brain telegraphs that such and such will substitute, and away you go. Then there are various tricks of working that help, too. You sieve dried egg as well as flour, because it's quicker to blend it smoothly when all the lumps are out. You warm fat before attempting to grease tins, and syrup before dipping in the spoon. You also warm the basin containing fat and sugar to be creamed; but not too much, as you don't want them to oil.

Having the various kinds of sugar displayed in labelled tins on a shelf over your working table saves time delving in the larder; so does getting icing sugar sieved, and dried fruit cleaned, whenever you have ten minutes to spare. Fruit cleaning, when you're working with your eye on the clock, is a nerve-racking business, but if the cleaned currants and sultanas, or ready-chopped raisins or dates, have only to be tipped out of a glass jar, the job can be taken in your stride.

THE CAKE FOR THE OCCASION.

It's important to have a choice of recipes, because sometimes a cake made by one method can be fitted in easier than another kind. For instance, if you have just half an hour to spare, from start to finish, a plain or chocolate sponge sandwich is as good a choice as any. It will only need 10–15 minutes to bake, so it won't occupy the oven for long. The ingredients are few, and no big mixing-bowl is necessary, so getting ready and clearing away are soon done. If you haven't the eggs and sugar necessary for the sponge to spare, some quick little cakes of the rock-cake or scone type would be most suitable. Remember, the smaller the proportion of fat to flour, the less time it takes to rub in. That's why plain cakes or pastry, when made this way, are always quicker than rich ones.

There's another advantage about the rubbed-in method. The work needn't all be done at once. Sometimes cooking a hot lunch on Sunday morning is a hectic rush. Well, the pastry for the fruit pie and the jam tarts can be part prepared overnight. Measure out ingredients; sift the dry ones. Rub in the fat finely. Flour the tins for the tartlets. If bottled fruit is being used for the pie, open it and put it ready in the pie dish, with sugar as necessary. Raw fruit can be prepared and part cooked, unless of a very soft kind.

One of the easiest types of cakes to prepare is the 'boil bake' or saucepan method one. All the ingredients, with the exception of the flour, are put in a saucepan and brought to the boil. After boiling for a while, usually ten minutes, during which time the mixture must be stirred, it is put on one side to cool. When cool, the flour is folded in and the cake baked. This cake can be done in three stages if more convenient. First, it might be overnight, dried fruit, sugar, fat, spices and baking soda are weighed or measured out, and prepared if necessary. Next morning, perhaps immediately after washing the breakfast dishes, the liquid is added and the mixture put on to boil. It is then left to cool while the rooms or shopping are done. When you come back to the kitchen to prepare the midday meal, for which you're going to use the oven, the flour is added and the cake baked.

Whether the mixture is put in an ordinary cake tin, a shallower Yorkshire pudding tin, or into individual ones, will depend on what else is cooking. If the oven is on rather low for a casserole, the deep cake is chosen, for the temperatures needed will coincide most closely. Supposing a hot-pot, wanting a moderately hot oven to brown off the potatoes, is cooking, then the shallower cake is the most profitable. On the other hand, if the oven is to be on for a short while only, but at a high temperature, it would be less trouble and most economical, to bake the mixture in little cake tins.

If you favour doing cakes by the 'creamed' method you'll know that what takes most time is adding the flour. This being so, it's best to leave big cakes for days when you're not rushed, and do little Queen cakes, or a Victoria sponge that can be cut in fingers and iced later if liked, for other occasions.

JAM MAKING IN YOUR STRIDE.

Jam making can be a hot and bothersome business, or a rather pleasant change from the usual routine. Even if you don't really enjoy it, or haven't time to devote best part of a day to it, you can still keep the tea-table supplied with home-made preserves without too much trouble. Don't try to tackle too big a quantity at once. *Do* understand something of the whys and wherefores of jam making before you start. It makes the whole process more interesting, and simpler, too.

Three things affect the setting qualities of jam—pectin, acid and water. All fruits contain pectin, a natural gum-like substance, but in very different amounts. Strawberries, cherries, blackberries and marrow have very little; currants, gooseberries and under-ripe plums contain a much larger proportion; so do apples. To bring the pectin into solution the fruit must be softened by cooking. The time taken to do this will depend upon the variety of fruit and its condition. When under-ripe or just ripe it contains more pectin than when over-ripe.

When to Add the Sugar.

The time to add the sugar is when a sufficient amount of pectin has been set free. If the moment is judged correctly, the jam will then require only a short period of boiling before it sets. The advantage of a short boil, apart from the time, fuel and effort saved, is that the colour and flavour of the fruit are preserved. Also as the jam has been reduced less by evaporation, the 'yield' will be better.

Acid or Pectin Extract for Poor-set Fruit.

Acid comes into the picture because it acts on the pectin during the cooking and makes it readily soluble. This is why in jam making an acid fruit is often combined with a sweet, acid-deficient one. Strawberry jam tends to be 'runny', but strawberry and gooseberry will set splendidly. Instead of adding an acid fruit, acid in the form of citric or tartaric acid may be used. There is a further alternative: to add natural or commercial pectin to the pectin-deficient fruits. You can get good natural pectin extract from sour apples—including windfalls, cores, skin and all—or from gooseberry or red-currant juice. Commercial pectin, in powder or liquid form, is obtainable from time to time.

The moisture-content of the fruit is the third factor affecting the set of the jam. Beginners sometimes add too much water to the fruit, or alternatively don't allow enough to evaporate during boiling, before adding the sugar. Tough-skinned fruit must be cooked long enough to become tender. Sufficient water must be allowed for this, but not too much, else the excess moisture won't have become absorbed by the time the cooking is finished. Some soft fruit won't need any water added at all. This is often the case during a damp season or when the fruit was picked when wet from rain. On the other hand, in a dry season, it may be necessary to add some water in order to soften the fruit sufficiently for the pectin to be set free.

So you see that with these 'variables' in the type and quality of fruit, jam-making recipes can't be hard and fast. Even the old hand will seldom produce two batches *exactly* the same. So don't be worried if your jam won't always set as it should. It will be eatable all right; and next time, if you benefit from the experience gained, you should be able to sail ahead.

THE 'METHYLATED' TEST.

One useful aid, until you have the confidence born of experience, is the methylated spirit test for pectin presence. All you need is a little glass jar, such as a fish-paste one, and a few teaspoonfuls of methylated spirit. When, according to the recipe, the fruit should be sufficiently cooked and ready for the addition of the sugar, bring to the boil for a moment or two. Then put a teaspoonful of the pulpy juice into the jar and, when cold, add three teaspoonfuls of 'meths'. Shake the jar a little so that the contents are mixed. If the pectin has been liberated in the juice, a transparent, jelly-like clot will form. In this case, the sugar can be added straight away. If the clot is not very firm, but appears in one or two lumps, or worse still, if there are only small globules, cook longer, at boiling point.

Remember that over-cooking reduces the pectin content, so test as soon as the fruit seems ready. If a good deal of water had to be added, as with gooseberries or black currants, the liquid should have been reduced, and the skins should be thoroughly tender before testing. Adding the sugar will tend rather to harden than soften skins. If after three tests the pectin still does not appear satisfactory, the only thing to do is to add some pectin-rich fruit, or pectin extract or acid before the sugar goes in. But, if you had a reliable recipe, this should seldom be necessary, so don't worry!

HOW LONG TO BOIL.

The only other point about jam making likely to cause worry is wondering whether it has been boiled long enough after the sugar has been added. If the pectin test has been followed successfully, boil *hard* for the shortest time given in the recipe, and not more than ten minutes for any jam. Then test by pouring a little of the syrup into a cold saucer and when cool drawing the finger across the surface to see whether the skin wrinkles. After one or two jam-making attempts, it's often possible to tell by the way the liquid boils. If large bubbles appear and the froth dies away, it is probably ready. Even so, do the saucer drill!

Once you have the 'feel' of jam making, you will not find it difficult to 'work in' small batches without upsetting the daily routine. Making a large quantity at once is doubtful wisdom unless you can concentrate on that alone. Not only does it mean a long time spent on preparing the fruit, but handling a big preserving pan, and measuring out the boiling jam is hot, rather tiring work. In contrast, a saucepanful can often be poured straight into the jars and sealed down in between doing other cooking jobs, without much extra effort.

Spread over Two Days if Easier.

Don't hesitate to split up the preparation if more convenient. Top and tail gooseberries or stone plums overnight, getting the family to help if you can. If fruit is soft and mushy, put on to cook straight away. It's not essential, however, to add the sugar and finish off the jam all in one bout. The cooked fruit can be left for a few hours, or even overnight, without harm. When you want to resume, bring the contents of the pan to the boil before adding the sugar.

Be Prepared with Equipment.

Always have equipment ready to use. See that jars are bone dry as well as clean before putting away. They will then only need rinsing in hot water before sterilising in the oven. Keep in stock covers of various sizes, for there's nothing more exasperating than having to cut down waxed circles when the jam is waiting to be potted.

TAKING THE DRUDGERY OUT OF FRUIT BOTTLING.

Fruit bottling is something at which it pays to be proficient, especially to-day. At first it seems a tedious, weary job, but with experience it gets less and less exacting. Again, take care that jars are dried off before storing away. Go over the stock of caps and rings at the beginning of the season and get necessary renewals. Check up that everything is in order before ever you get your fruit. The preparation—stringing currants, topping the gooseberries, removing maggots from blackberries—takes the most time, so try to get help with this. Unless the fruit is soft and in poor condition it can be prepared overnight and sterilised in the morning.

If you concentrate on one method, your actions will more quickly become automatic. With a proper sterilising outfit, the under-water method is simplest. Without it, the oven way. If you're short of time, bottle in water rather than in syrup if the oven method is being used. It makes no difference to the keeping qualities of the fruit, and little or none to the flavour. Don't worry if the fruit flies to the top of the bottles and stays crammed there instead of distributing itself equally. It means you have over-sterilised a little. It detracts from the appearance, but from nothing else. On the other hand, be sure to give tomatoes considerably longer than fruit. If under-sterilised, they will not keep.

By the time you have made one or two batches of jam and bottled enough fruit to carry the family through next winter, you will know well enough whether chutney making or pickling should be attempted. Unless there is produce from the garden crying out to be used, it's probably not worth the work involved, except in the case of making tomato sauce or purée, which is so valuable in the winter. If you do decide to have a go, study the chutney and pickle recipes to find one that fits in both with the ingredients you have to hand and also the amount of time at your disposal. With a free afternoon, making a cooked confection like chutney will seem a good idea. Pickles which need brining can be spread over a couple of days or more, so if it's a question of having an odd hour or two, they will be the wiser venture.

Chapter XIV

DOING THE WASHING

ASKED what she found the most exhausting part of running the home, a very efficient single-handed housewife replied without a moment's hesitation: "Oh, the washing." Prior to her marriage, nearly twenty years ago, she had taken a short course in domestic economy. She knew the right way to tackle every household job, and took a pride in doing them all well. Yet with all her practice she still finds Monday an ordeal. One reason is that her equipment is so poor. Her single sink, with one draining-board only, is placed in a corner. The wash-boiler, of the round type, won't take a wringer. She could get a new kind of wringer that would fasten to the edge of the sink (*see* Appendix I, p. 192), but she makes do with the old one that must be lugged in from the garden shed each time. It is fastened on to a rickety stand which has to be steadied with a chair-back if it's not to sway and shake, with the risk of collapsing entirely. On a bright day she can get the clothes dry in the garden; otherwise, there's the misery of lots of wet things flapping round the little kitchenette, for she has no drying cabinet of any kind.

Doing a big wash, and the home-maker in question copes with everything for her husband and two schoolboy sons as well as her own things and most of the household linen, is certainly drudgery in such circumstances. Yet with laundries as expensive as they are to-day, and sometimes unreliable into the bargain, it's little wonder that many a middle-class housewife decides that she must buckle to and do the job herself.

THE EQUIPMENT QUESTION.

If this is the case, there's no doubt that some capital expenditure on the right tools is well worth while. The only essentials for home laundry work are hot water, cleansing agents, a good deep sink and washbowls, a wringer and some kind of boiler. The latter may be quite small, to go on the top of a stove, or it may be an independently-heated affair.

To cut down time and effort, improvements on this minimum equipment must be made. For instance, one of the heaviest jobs is taking wet things from the sink to the wringer, and then back again for rinsing. If the clothes can be put through the wringer without moving them away from the spot where they have been washed, so they go straight into a rinsing bowl on the other side, tiring labour, mess and time will be saved.

In some of the newer homes, the wash-boiler or washing machine is built in next to the sink. It has a wringer that can be folded down under a table-top when not in use, or easily detached and stored away. Other recently built houses have a separate, independently-heated sink next to the ordinary one, or a double sink, to the middle bar of which a detachable wringer can be fixed. Unfortunately, the great majority of kitchens don't offer any of these amenities. Almost equally effective, is the square portable wash-boiler or washing machine, with attached folding wringer, which can be moved flush up to the sink.

In the last year, a fair number of hand-operated simple washing machines of this type have come into the shops. They are really only an elaboration of a wash-boiler, but quite a useful one. The machine is filled, by means of rubber tubing, from the kitchen tap. The water is then heated to the temperature required by gas or electricity, depending on the make of machine. Clothes can be left to soak, boiled up if necessary, or mechanically washed by means of a hand-operated 'agitator'. They are then wrung into the kitchen sink for rinsing. Further details of some of these machines are given in Appendix I, p. 190.

For those who can afford the capital outlay, anything from £30 to £100, as against the £20 or less cost of the simple type described above, the electric washer cuts down time and fatigue still further. On the other hand, some mechanical washing machines take a certain amount of time to get ready and clean out again, so that unless the wash is family sized they may not prove such a good proposition.

The most expensive type on the market is operated on a different principle from the rest. It really does do all the job, from washing the clothes to cleaning and emptying itself after the laundry has been automatically rinsed and 'spin-dried'. On the other hand, quite considerable plumbing work is required for the installation, and the machine, which is not portable, takes up a fair amount of space. It pays best when the weekly wash is a fairly large one. Details of an automatic 'home laundry' now on the market are given in Appendix I, p. 191.

If you have an automatic washing machine you'll work according to the instructions given by the maker. Otherwise, whether you use a hand machine or a wash-boiler, or simply the kitchen sink or the bathroom wash-bowl, the job is made easier and more satisfying, too, if you follow a good method.

SORT THE CLOTHES.

Step one is to collect everything to be washed, and then to sort it. Preferably do this overnight. Put woollies in one pile, silks, rayons, and lightly soiled delicate cottons in another. Keep handkerchiefs separate and also the rest of the cottons and linens. Sort these again in order of dirtiness. Such things as net curtains which will probably have a lot of dust in them are best put on their own.

WHEN TO SOAK.

Overnight soaking in cold water, with, if liked, a little borax or ammonia added to soften it, will help considerably with the curtains and also with other cottons where the soiling is of a dusty rather than a greasy nature. Perspiration-soiled garments, such as shirts, are also the better for a soaking in cold water in which borax has been dissolved. Don't soak 'coloureds' that might 'run', or silks or woollens of any kind. Handkerchiefs should have salt added to the soaking water. Keep them separate from the rest.

While you are sorting for soaking, deal with any stains. Cold salt water is best for blood or meat juice; hot water and borax for tea, coffee or fruit. Other stains, with detailed methods for removal, are dealt with in Appendix II, pp. 203–205.

A CHOICE OF CLEANSING AGENTS.

When you are ready to wash, collect water softener, if you live in a hard-water district, soap, soap powder or flakes, soapless cleaner, laundry blue and if it is to be used, starch.

A water softener will make soap go further, and if used carefully can't hurt the clothes. Soda is the cheapest, but it *must* be dissolved completely in the water before soap is added. Safest plan is to make a bottled solution, dissolve two ounces of washing soda in one quart of water and allow to cool before using. London water, containing twenty degrees of hardness, needs two tablespoonfuls of the solution per gallon. Ammonia and borax will also soften water quite efficiently. Soapless cleansers, in both powder or liquid form, work equally well in hard or soft water. While excellent for woollies, lightly soiled silks and rayons and fine stockings, most of these 'washers' are not recommended for really dirty articles. But they are very satisfactory for part of the laundry work to-day, for, as well as being unrationed, articles washed in them do not shrink. Providing a good brand is chosen it will pay especially to use these cleansers for woollies.

Whether you use soap powder, a jelly made from shredded washing soap, soap flakes or bar soap, is mainly a question of taste. For whites and dirty cotton materials, a good soap powder, with perhaps a rub of bar soap for very dirty parts, such as shirt collars, is a favourite choice. For silks, rayons and woollies, pure soap flakes or good soap jelly tend to be safer.

METHODS OF WASHING.

Some people find it convenient to have two or more 'lots' of washing going at once. For instance, after any overnight soaking, the cottons, in order of dirtiness, are put into hot soapy water in the wash-boiler. The more delicate ones are washed through straight away, the rest are left to soak, or, if necessary, brought up to the boil. The most soiled clothes are added last, probably with extra soap powder. In the meantime, woollies may be sudsed in soapless cleaner, or rayons and silks washed through in warm soapy lather made with mild soapflakes or soap jelly. Never use water hotter than the hand can comfortably bear for woollens, rayons or silks.

Other equally experienced and successful home launderers prefer to use the same type of soap throughout, and to have only one sink, or wash-boiler, in action. In this case, silks, rayons and woollies are tackled first, while the water is not too hot. Then come the cottons in order of dirtiness, with hotter water and more soap. This method may be a little more economical in both hot water and soap, but it's largely a question of what suits your individual circumstances the better.

Whichever attack you find the more convenient, remember that delicate fabrics, which means mainly silk, woollens and rayons, should never be rubbed, but rather kneaded and squeezed. Rubbing in time frays the threads and, with woollens especially, causes matting of the fibres and felting.

RINSING AND WRINGING.

Rinsing is very important. Water of the same temperature as used for washing is safest, especially with woollens. Cottons can be rinsed in cold, for the second or third water at least. If possible, pass through a wringer before, as well as after, rinsing. This will take out a good deal of the lime scum which causes the ugly grey marks on silks and woollens.

When the rinsing water is perfectly clear, pass clothes through the wringer again. Fold the articles lengthwise, and be careful of buttons and fastenings. If you have no wringing machine, squeeze out as much water as possible by hand, but don't twist silks, rayons or woollies. Wrap them in a Turkish towel; quite a lot more moisture will be absorbed. Flat drying, in a clothes-hammock for instance, is recommended for woollies, such as jumpers, that are likely to drop. On a blowy, quick-drying day they can be put on a clothes-hanger on the line. Don't dry any delicate fabrics in strong sunlight. Silks and rayons can be pegged to dry so long as they are not too heavy. Rayons, especially, are often 'tender' when wet, so take special care. In many ways, the safest way for silk or rayon undies or other 'smalls' is to wrap in a towel until dry enough to iron. They must not become bone dry.

THE 'BOILING' QUESTION.

"Is it necessary to boil?" is a question that worries a good many novices. Generally speaking, dirt can be removed by soaking and careful washing. Boiling does have a certain purifying and whitening effect on sheets, table linen and similar 'whites', and it's also recommended for handkerchiefs, at least every now and again. For the latter, or for tea-towels if they are done at home, a small boiler which can be placed on top of the stove is useful. Wash and rinse the handkerchiefs in the usual way, then bring *slowly* to the boil in soapy water in which a little borax has been dissolved. It's the stewing that has the whitening effect.

BLEACHING, BLUEING AND STIFFENING.

The question of bleaching won't generally arise if clothes are dried out of doors, preferably in the sunlight, and boiled occasionally. This is especially so if whites are 'blued'. Do this immediately after rinsing, testing the water with a piece of rag if you're not sure of the strength. Don't leave the clothes lying in the blue water, else they will tend to become dyed instead of just having the yellowness corrected. If table linen or tea-towels need rather more drastic treatment to make them look snowy, use one of the good commercial bleaches occasionally. Follow instructions given on the bottle and never use a stronger solution than required.

Starching gives the finishing touch to table linen, shirts, cotton frocks and overalls, while a very mild solution improves net curtains and muslin blouses. Directions for making starch are usually given on the packet. In general, mix with cold water in the proportion of one part of starch to three parts of water. Then pour on boiling water until the starch clears. This full-strength starch solution must then be diluted according to the stiffness required. Stiff collars, for instance, require it 'neat', while shirts, dresses and blouses will need a solution of about one part of starch only to eight parts of water. Table linen comes in between, according to the stiffness you prefer. The secret of starching is to get the articles evenly saturated. Immerse them in the starch water, after washing, one at a time, moving about all the time. Then wring carefully by hand, so that the excess starch is squeezed off. Dry completely and then 'damp down' before ironing. To do this, spread out each article on a table and sprinkle with warm water. Remember, *sprinkle.* Hit or miss methods don't work here! A flour dredger, kept for the purpose, or a bottle with a hole in the cork, make excellent sprinklers. Then roll up tightly, smoothing into shape as you do so.

Sometimes silks would be improved by a little stiffening, or old veils or fine muslins need a crisper finish. For them, a rinsing in gum-arabic solution is the thing. Get the gum-arabic crystals at a chemist's. Put in a jar with water, in the proportion of four ounces of crystals to one pint, and heat till dissolved by standing the jar in a saucepan of water over a moderate heat. Strain through muslin, and bottle. Dilute one or two teaspoonfuls with half a pint of water, or even use a stronger solution, for the rinsing. Iron while still damp.

IRONING.

Washing is only the half of home laundry. Ironing is the other. Some things, such as silk, rayon, or nylon stockings should never be ironed. Others, including all stockings and socks, woollen underwear and men's cellular or knitted-type cotton underwear, needn't be, if time is an important factor. At the most, all such articles need is 'touching up', providing they are well dried and aired. This applies, too, to Turkish towels, which can be run over after the current is switched off and the rest of the ironing finished.

As with washing, good equipment can take most of the

drudgery out of ironing. A folding ironing board is immeasurably more satisfactory than a table, and a sleeve board, though not so necessary, does help in obtaining a good finish. The choice of irons to-day is large. An electric iron is to be preferred, but there are gas models too, which can be used with 'bottled' gas, if necessary. If an old-fashioned flat iron has to be used, do at least have a detachable 'shoe'. If you are buying an electric iron, try to have a heat-controlled one. An excellent make is available at about £2, suitable for A.C. and D.C. mains. (*See* Appendix I, p. 193.) The advantage of a heat-controlled iron lies in there being no need to stop frequently to switch off and on in order to regulate the heat. The *correct* temperature is maintained for whatever type of fabric is being ironed. Rayons, woollens and silks need, in that order, a cooler iron than cottons or linens. With a heat-controlled iron, risk of scorching is almost eliminated, while the amount of current used is cut to the minimum.

Apart from the temperature differences, fabrics need special treatment according to the fibre and the finish. Except for woollens, over which a damp cloth is placed, and tussore silk, which is rare now, all materials should be slightly damp. While cottons and linens are best 'damped down' by sprinkling, after having dried completely, silks and rayons should be ironed before they are quite dry. Damping them down may mean unsightly water-marks, so if the clothes have gone too dry it's better to dip them into water again and to squeeze in a towel rather than sprinkling with water.

Generally speaking, silks and rayons of whatever type should be ironed on the wrong side, cottons and linens on the right. With material that shrinks up in washing, such as georgettes and some kinds of crêpes, you want to iron lengthwise first and then across the weave, pulling out carefully as you go. Practice, and careful experiment with the underside of a hem that does not show, will indicate whether it is safe to finish off rayon or silk on the right side. If this is done, a cooler iron is advisable. Always iron double parts first and then work from the least easily creased to the most noticeable parts. For instance, after doing shoulder pads, yoke or other double parts, including seams of a dress, go on to the sleeves, next the shoulders. Take the back and then the front of the bodice next before going on to the skirt. Finally, do lapels, buttonholes and hem, and any touching up necessary.

Take it easily, and don't get discouraged if at first you crease up again almost as quickly as you smooth out! After a little practice you'll get the trick of arranging the clothes over the board to the best advantage. Never fold while still warm unless, like a shirt or handkerchief, you want the folds to be ironed in. Although the iron itself is weighty, you want a light hand. As with pastry making, it will come!

HOW TO FIT IN THE LAUNDRY WORK.

So much for the general technique of home laundry work. But how to fit it into the weekly routine? The usual plan, of course, is to make Monday washing day. In households where this is done, cooking and housework are usually cut to a minimum then. The obvious advantage is that less hot water and soap are used than if the work were split up. Time is saved, too, if equipment has to be got out and assembled, while there's a certain satisfaction in feeling that the whole job has to be 'polished off' at one time.

Against this, there's little doubt that a good deal of the dislike of clothes washing comes from the fact that attempting too much at once results in over-tiredness. Washing, done with a plentiful supply of hot water, soap and other adequate tools, is not unpleasant in itself. In fact, many people derive considerable satisfaction from it. It's clean work, the results do show, and, although it demands intelligent care, it doesn't absorb the whole of one's attention all the time.

When one is working against the clock and there is a good

deal of lifting of wet clothes and bending over a sink with consequent back-ache, the pleasanter aspects of the work tend to disappear, and on come the 'wash-day blues'. This is particularly so in bad weather, when to the washing difficulties are added those of getting the things dried. Drying cabinets, unfortunately, are still rather a luxury. (*See* Appendix I, p. 192.)

So perhaps the best plan is to decide according to circumstances whether it's better to concentrate on getting it all done in a single swoop, or to split the wash into several parts. In the latter case, a good method is to do at one time all the 'whites' or clothes that need soaking or boiling, but to wash through 'smalls', personal lingerie and so forth, in several batches during the week. For instance, if you have your bath at night, mix up a little lather in the lavatory basin and put in stockings and undies. They will only need squeezing through after you've bathed; and rinsing, wrapping in a towel to remove excess moisture and hanging to dry won't take more than a few minutes.

Where there are small children in the family, some washing will be a daily chore. Napkins must be put to steep in cold water immediately after use. They will probably have to be washed out twice daily, perhaps after tea and after breakfast. After the breakfast dishes are done is a good time for washing the children's clothing. Woollies can be washed through straight away; cotton frocks left to soak while the beds are being made. Whatever system you adopt, make it a regular 'drill', so that doing it becomes second nature. Of course, time will be saved if the wringer can be left fixed up ready for use, and if there is a spare sink or basin that can be utilised for soaking, so try to arrange this.

SIMPLIFY IF NECESSARY.

If washing has to be done daily, some of the refinements will have to go. Cut out starching as much as possible, and don't iron anything that can get by without it. When shopping for new things, think of the amount of laundry work they will mean as well as whether they are good value, attractive, hard wearing and so forth. Cellular-type shirts and underwear can cut down washing and ironing time appreciably during the summer months, when almost daily changes are required. Nylon or rayon mesh need less ironing than crêpes, satins or ninons; dresses of the seersucker type take much less time to get up than most other cottons or linens. Little girls' muslin frocks with frills and smocking look adorable, but simple styles give Mother more time to be out of doors with the children. All these things must be considered by the single-handed home-maker.

When the ironing is done will again depend upon the individual case. If you are up bright and early on Monday morning, get away to a good start and polish off the wash by lunch-time, you'll probably like to go straight ahead and get the ironing through before it's time to think about the evening meal. When there are children to be taken out in the afternoon, or it was not possible to get the clothes washed and dried by midday, ironing will have to be an evening job.

In this case, make it as pleasant as possible. Do it in one of the sitting-rooms, where you can talk to the family or listen to the radio. In fact, a popular way is to fit the ironing in to coincide with a radio programme you want to hear. Then have a stool (the kitchen one usually answers well) of convenient height for the board, and do all except the special bits sitting down. This cuts out much of the fatigue, and doesn't slow up the work very much. Handled this way, ironing can be a job that gives the satisfaction obtained from doing fine handwork, without taking you away from the family circle or preventing mental relaxation as well.

Chapter XV

DOING THE MENDING

To many women, mending proves particularly irksome. It's not that they dislike needlework in itself, but in recent years they've had too big a dose of unrewarding work on things that have gone too far. No wonder they find it impossible to get any satisfaction out of what can be quite a pleasant job. Now that goods are not in such short supply, don't let mending become a bugbear. It's truer economy to discard than to squander precious time for results that don't last anyway, especially as practically everything can be utilised for some other purpose.

Of course it requires determination, but try to do first-aid to torn things before they are washed or sent to the laundry, and to tackle regular repairs before putting the articles back ready for use again. An evening's work firmly devoted to the mending basket really does pay. Make a date with the wireless, and do your darning to 'Saturday Night Theatre' or some other favourite. Alternatively, a regular sewing afternoon when a friend comes to tea with *her* mending bag, is a good idea.

Applying the correct treatment will prove worth while, too. Although machining a patch on a worn sheet will often answer, it would be disastrous on, say, flannel trousers. Darning a thin place saves future work, but when it's a question of a hole, a patch usually proves quicker.

Whether you darn or patch, cover enough of the thin material round the actual hole or thin part. Otherwise the strain on the old material will cause a fresh weakness and your work will go for nothing. Don't use new stuff for a patch if it can be avoided. The ideal is a piece of material taken from the underside of the garment, or from inside a pocket. With household mending, try to find a piece suitable for a patch amongst similarly worn material. If the stuff has to be new, wash it first.

DARNING.

Special points are: (1) to take care not to pull the article out of shape either by dragging stitches too tightly or by letting the darn itself 'bag'; (2) to keep the shape of the darn irregular so that the strain of the new threads is distributed evenly; (3) to allow for shrinking of the new yarn by leaving loops to the threads and (4) to work with thread of a texture, as well as colour, as close as possible to the original. As a general rule, darns are done on the wrong side. Sometimes, when mending a woollen dress material with threads drawn from the hem or selvedge, it will be easier to follow the original weave if the darn is done on the right side. The loops at the end of each line must then be taken through to the back. When darning a large hole, a piece of net, tacked over the hole first, saves time and makes a stronger job of it, too.

For a simple darn, begin working on the wrong side, beyond the thin part of the material, doing the selvedge or

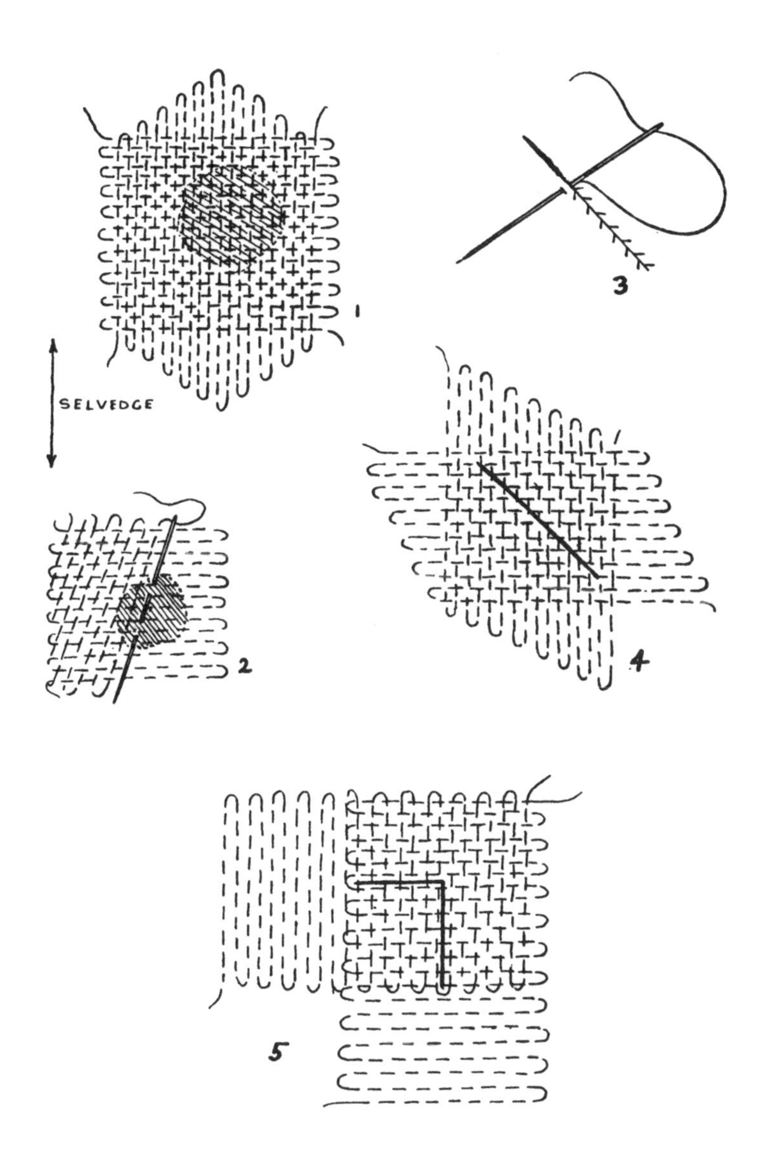
1
SELVEDGE
2
3
4
5

warp threads first. Then work in the opposite direction, picking up the threads across the hole as in weaving. Take care not to split the darning thread (diagram 1). If some elasticity is wanted, say over a stocking knee, a diagonal darn is preferable (diagram 2).

Knife-cut and Hedge-tear Darns.

To darn a tear or knife cut, first draw the edges together with what is known as a fishbone stitch (diagram 3). Then darn diagonally across in either direction (diagram 4). For a right-angled, or hedge tear, draw the edges together as before. Then, starting at the outside edge, darn across one side of the tear. Turn the work round and darn in a similar manner across the other side. There will thus be a double square of darning in the angle where the material is weakest (diagram 5).

PATCHING.

Remember that: (1) the patch must follow the line of the warp and weft of the material, or else it will be very noticeable; (2) the patch should preferably be a square or an oblong; (3) it's best to unpick seams or hems near to the hole so that the patch can be carried to the hem or seam and one edge inserted in it; (4) corners need special care; (5) tacking the patch into position first makes it easier to sew evenly with no puckering or stretching; (6) matching the thread carefully makes the patch less noticeable.

The Calico and Flannel Patches.

The most commonly used patches are known as the calico, the print and the flannel patch respectively. With the calico and the flannel patch, the right side of the patch is placed against the wrong side of the material. There are two rows of visible stitching. These patches are firm and straightforward to do, and are right for most household repairs and for underwear. For silk stuffs, as well as cottons, the calico patch is correct; for woollens, one naturally uses the flannel patch.

With a calico patch, either oversew or machine on the wrong side. Then turn to the right side of the garment and neatly snip away the ragged material to within five-eighths of an inch of the stitching. Snip each corner a quarter of an inch and fold this amount under for a turning. Stitch down neatly. The same method is used for a flannel patch except that no turnings are necessary and herringbone stitch is used on both sides (diagrams 6 and 7).

THE PRINT PATCH.

A print patch is used for a patterned fabric, and also for materials where a patch that shows as little as possible is required. Use it for any fabrics except heavy woollens. It is done on the right side. Take great care in matching the design on a patterned material, and the weave on a plain one, and use small, unobtrusive stitches. Allow three-eighths-of-an-inch turnings. On the wrong side, the material round the hole is cut away and neatened with blanket stitching, so one row of stitches only shows on the right side (diagram 8).

THE TAILOR'S SEWN PATCH.

For a heavy woollen material, a tailor's sewn patch is worth the trouble. With this, the material is inserted, rather than applied. On the wrong side, mark the square of worn or thin material to be patched, using tailor's chalk and a ruler. Cut the patch three-eighths of an inch larger all the way round. Mark with chalk on the wrong side of the patch the exact size of the square. On the garment, cut along the marked line on one side of the square and insert one side of the patch through the slit so that the raw edges are level. You will have to fold back the three-eighths-of-an-inch turning on the patch at each end of this first side in order to pull it through the slit smoothly. Take care that the right side of the patch

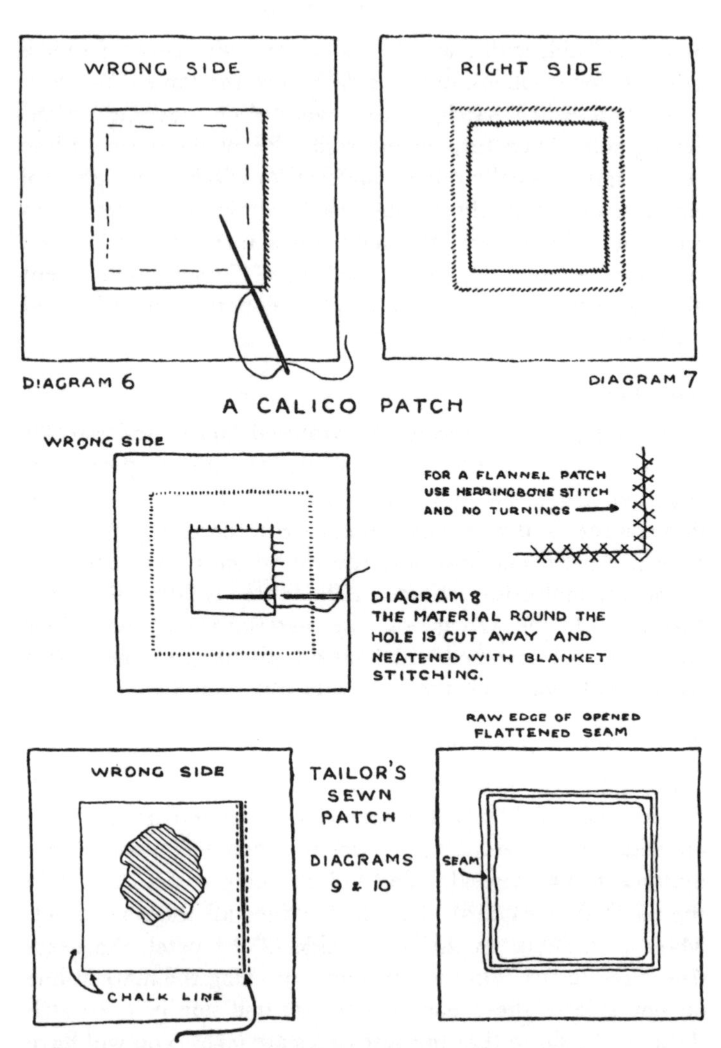
WRONG SIDE
RIGHT SIDE
DIAGRAM 6
DIAGRAM 7
A CALICO PATCH
WRONG SIDE
FOR A FLANNEL PATCH
USE HERRINGBONE STITCH
AND NO TURNINGS
DIAGRAM 8
THE MATERIAL ROUND THE
HOLE IS CUT AWAY AND
NEATENED WITH BLANKET
STITCHING.
RAW EDGE OF OPENED
FLATTENED SEAM
WRONG SIDE
TAILOR'S
SEWN
PATCH
DIAGRAMS
9 & 10
SEAM
CHALK LINE
INSERT PATCH THROUGH SLOT ON ONE SIDE. STITCH PATCH AND
GARMENT TOGETHER 3/8" WIDTH FROM CUT EDGE OF GARMENT AND ALONG
CHALK LINE ON PATCH. CONTINUE CUTTING ALONG LINE AND INSERTING PATCH.

is on the right side of the garment. Tack firmly together along the chalk line on the patch, and at a distance of three-eighths of an inch from the cut edge of the garment. Continue cutting along the sides of the marked hole and inserting the patch. The corners need special care; see that they are not rounded but form a right angle. When tacked exactly in position, backstitch firmly with good sewing silk, or machine if you can manage it. Then cut off the corners, spread open the seam and press flat, using a damp cloth and a moderately hot iron (diagrams 9 and 10).

Patching Net Curtains.

An unconventional type of patching, useful for torn net curtains, becomes possible again now that rice has returned to the market. Save the water in which it has been cooked and use it to stick a fresh piece of net over the torn part. Place the curtain on your ironing-board or on a table with a blanket beneath. Dip the material to be used for repair into the rice water, wring out well, place it over the hole and press with a hot iron. The join will scarcely show and much time will be saved.

MAKING OVER HOUSEHOLD LINENS.

Quite apart from darning and patching there are various ways of dealing with worn household linens. Slit sheets down the middle and seam the sides together before the centre has worn too thin. The new sides will have to be finished with a hem, which means that the re-made sheets will be somewhat smaller than the old, but they will do for 'bottoms', or for a smaller bed. Sometimes it's the hems or corners that get torn. If so, reinforcing with tape is effective and simple. Draw the torn edges together and darn lightly. Then stitch the tape on to the wrong side of the sheet, with a row of stitching at each edge of the tape. Mitre the corners neatly, and be sure to allow enough tape to more than cover the worn part. This type of repair is also suitable for towels or to reinforce a torn buttonhole.

When sheets, towels or pillow-cases have gone too far, the only wise course is to cut them up and use the good parts in other ways. Cut down bath towels for kitchen ones. The best parts of two thin Turkish towels machined together will make a bath mat; little pieces make face-cloths. Remaining strips and odd shapes come in handy for cleaning rags. Sheets too far gone for turning 'sides to middle' will cut up into bolster cases, and under pillow-slips. Biggish pieces of *linen* sheets or pillow-slips, placed double and machined together, are useful as drying-up cloths. Keep odd strips for bandages.

FIRST AID TO SHIRTS.

In the realm of clothes, it's repairs to shirts that are likely to give the most trouble. Even though the coupon worry is no more, the high prices make many a professional and

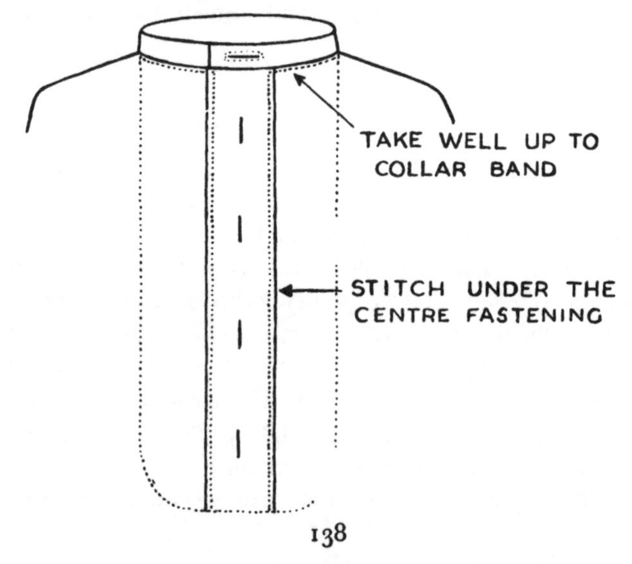

business man think twice before buying new. Shirt fronts usually show signs of wear first. A neat darn may answer for a very tiny hole, but, as a rule, it's best to sacrifice the shirt tail, which can be made good with a piece from a still older garment, and cover the front with a fresh dickey. Cut two pieces large enough to fit the front of the shirt from the curve of the neckline to below the opening of the waistcoat. Turn in narrow turns, tack and then stitch neatly into position. It should be possible to hide the front row of stitches with the narrow overlap of the front opening. The curved edge beneath the collar band wants most care. Don't cut away the old shirt beneath unless it is very ragged, as the extra thickness of material will help save wear.

With a collar-attached shirt, the collar itself is usually the first casualty. A quick method is to unpick the collar and reverse it. The drawbacks to this are that if the collar is turned up, as with a tennis shirt, the frayed reverse side will show. Also, some collars have tabs stitched to the reverse side to take stiffeners. These will have to be unpicked, and the material beneath will probably look a little brighter than the rest. A visit to the laundry will soon adjust this. An alternative way of dealing with the collar is to cover it with a piece of material cut from the shirt tail. Cut a straight piece of material rather wider than the deepest, pointed part of the collar. Tack into position at the neckband on the right side, allowing a turning. Machine over the original stitches on the wrong side. Then from the right side, shape the surplus material over the edge of the collar, turn down and stitch lightly into position. Cuffs can be done similarly, only as they are straight the alteration will be simpler.

Chapter XVI

KEEPING HOUSEHOLD ACCOUNTS AND BUDGETING

"ANNUAL income £20, annual expenditure £19 19s. 6d., result happiness. Annual income £20, annual expenditure £20 0s. 6d., result misery," pronounced Mr. Micawber. He may have simplified the matter, but the principle is not disputed. The difficulty lies in putting his recipe for happiness into practice. Perhaps the only way to do this is summed up in the words of a still older saying: "Cut your coat according to your cloth."

A 'PAPER PATTERN' TO FOLLOW.

The trouble is that one tends to think that the 'cloth' will go farther than is actually the case. So the best way to work is to have a paper pattern to follow; in other words, a budget. With your husband, write down all the items that must come out of your income. Rent, or mortgage repayments, and rates; electricity, gas and solid fuel; telephone; car costs;

dentist's bills; food; clothes; personal allowance for recreation; reading, cigarettes, etc.; a reserve for holidays; charity; emergencies. Even if all these don't concern you, the list is long enough. Against the fixed items put what you actually have to pay out; estimate what you think will be the yearly cost of the rest. You'll be remarkably lucky if your estimated expenditure comes within your income! Here is where the first paring down must come. At this stage, you and your husband will probably agree on the housekeeping allowance you can have, and what it must cover. Once this is decided, begin to work out a more detailed budget.

Expenditure on some items of food, such as meat and milk, are largely controlled by rationing. On the other hand, there's practically no limit to what you can spend at the greengrocer's or at the grocer's on unrationed items, if you have the money. So it is here you must decide what the top limit each week, or month, must be. Don't forget, when allocating your allowance, items such as household renewals, which includes anything from dish swabs to a new saucepan or fruit-bottling jars; occasional household help, if any; shoe repairs; laundry and dry cleaning, which usually come out of 'housekeeping'; the family's sweets, if you buy them; and the newsagent's and chemist's bills. Follow Mr. Micawber's advice in allowing a small reserve for emergencies or forgotten items. Even if you have a separate dress allowance, which will take in hair dressing or other personal expenditure, there are always trifles such as fares when out shopping, and postage, which if not allowed for can mount up disconcertingly.

WRITE DOWN ALL YOU SPEND.

You may think that such detail is unnecessary. It all depends upon the size of your allowance, though of course individual temperament has to be reckoned with as well. But when there is an ample margin, occasional 'lashing out' or poor planning doesn't matter so much. In all other cases, it's wise to accept the discipline of writing down, under the appropriate heading, every penny spent, and of checking it over, too, both with the budget and with other items. There's nothing more effective for nipping any extravagances in the bud than seeing the result down in black and white. By jotting down everything, you can spot at once not only whether you are keeping within bounds, but whether you are spending to the best advantage. The right balance must be held not only between expenditure on food and on other items, but on the various types of food. Your aim in the latter case will be to provide the best diet possible.

Because of this, what you spend on food, and how you budget it, must be flexible to a certain extent. Sometimes you must allot a larger proportion to the greengrocer's, as when oranges and grape-fruit are in season. Another time, you may have to get the necessary vitamin C by buying canned fruit juice, which means a necessary increase in what is spent at the grocer's. When fresh herrings or roes are in good supply, it would be folly to buy canned ones. During a rough spell when there is little at the fishmonger's you will have to fall back on 'points' fish. In the summer, when greens are cheap, you won't necessarily want more of them, though money may well be spent on fruit for bottling. If this is not available, spending for the store cupboard would be good economics. At all times bear in mind that the largest possible proportion should be spent on protective and builder foods, that is, those containing vitamins and protein. (*See* Chapter XI, pp. 96–8, on meal-planning.) If cuts must be made, pass by the pastrycook's rather than the dairy or the greengrocer's.

BUDGET YOUR TIME, TOO.

Finally, don't forget to place a value on your time, and to budget that, too. If there's a choice between making or buying

SUGGESTED A/C FORM FOR WEEKLY HOUSEKEEPING EXPENDITURE

	£	s.	d.
Housekeeping money received . . .			
Balance brought forward (or deficit owed) .			
Money in hand at beginning of week .			

	Wkly Budget	*Sun.*	*Mon.*	*Tues.*	*Wed.*	*Thurs.*	*Fri.*	*Sat.*	TOTAL
Baker									
Butcher									
Grocer									
Dairy									
Fishmonger									
Laundry and cleaning									
Stamps (postage and insurance)									
Chemist									
Household renewals									
Dress and personal									
Fares									
Recreation									
Miscellaneous									
							Total expenditure for week		
							Balance or deficit to be carried forward		

clothes, and the same with cakes and jam, decide which you do best, and most profitably. Weigh up the value of leisure, and the health and happiness a little more of it may give you—and those about you. Man does not live by bread alone, and the home-maker has more responsibilities than feeding the family well and keeping the home in good repair without running into debt.

Chapter XVII

ADAPTING THE ROUTINE WHEN BABY COMES

LET'S face it, the single-handed mother with children of under school age is the home-maker with the most on her plate. This is equally true if for children is substituted 'child', for an only one will exact more companionship from the mother than when two or more can help to amuse each other.

BEGIN BEFORE BABY COMES.

Half-way through the waiting months before the first baby comes, begin to streamline the household routine. You will have to make time for an afternoon rest, for a daily walk. Before your pregnancy, you probably found so many interesting things to do in your new home that you didn't give yourself this amount of leisure. Well, you manage to have the rest and the walk. It may mean cutting down on the quantity, or the quality and finish, of the laundry you do at home. Perhaps there is time for rather less entertaining, or at least it becomes simpler as you make fewer fancy cakes or experiment with new dishes. But with your new interests it doesn't seem to matter.

Make up your mind that this simplification of the business of living will have to continue, if not be intensified. There will be another person to cater for whose habits and needs will be quite different from those of you and your husband. The amount of clothes and bed-linen to be washed will take a steep upward turn. Extra demands will be made on your company and attention. Also, for a while at least, you may be less physically fit. However good a manager you are, and however naturally strong, one thing is certain. You'll wonder what on earth you found to do before the baby arrived!

So before he actually does appear, do sit down and think seriously about your methods. You'll be having a lot of additional calls on your time, so let's see whether some of your present work can't be eliminated altogether.

WHERE TO SAVE TIME.

First of all, *the daily tidying up*. Can you compress it into half an hour less, say, to make room for baby's morning bath? You and your husband may not be quite as careful as you could be about not making work. A little more strictness about using ash-trays, and emptying them overnight, about putting the room to rights, collecting newspapers and restoring books to their shelves, may save ten minutes in the morning.

What about the bathroom? Have you stuck to the vow you made of having a cloth and cleaner kept there, and both of you wiping down the bath after use? If not, now's the time to insist that this work-saving routine is carried out. A little more thoughtfulness about sloshing water about will cut down cleaning-up time, too. Men are the worst offenders here, and while we're on the subject, has your husband got slack about leaving his old razor blades on the shelf? It may only take a minute for you to clear them away, but minutes mount up!

It's civilised and pleasant to eat in the dining-room, if you have one, or in a niche in the sitting-room, but just now, can you justify the extra work entailed? Perhaps a folding table in the kitchen would be better. It shortens preparation a little, and means a little less clearing up in the sitting-room. When you do have two reception rooms, you may be able to use them alternately to save having to do two rooms each day.

Shopping time is well-spent if it means you're getting outdoor exercise and having some social contacts. But too much waiting about in shops, or queues, has nothing to commend it. It probably means you're not organising as well as you should. Check over where the precious minutes vanish fastest. If it's the grocer's, have a chat with the manager, or the assistant who normally serves you. Perhaps he could suggest a less busy day or time for you to call. Or if goods can't be delivered, perhaps you could drop the order in one day and pick up the goods the next. Then do you always make out a provisional order ahead? It may have to be adjusted according to supplies, but it does save humming and ha-ing in the shop. Getting fish is sometimes rather time-wasting. It may be worth arranging for a standing order once or twice a week, or perhaps you can take turns with a neighbour in going to the shop.

Cooking. Most husband-and-wife households make the evening meal the main event of the day. This means doing most of the cooking after an early tea. Now, an hour at least must be devoted to baby: 'topping and tailing', washing, feeding and some play before bed. Will it be better to dine at midday instead? It won't be very long before you will have to have a proper dinner for baby, so it may be as well to make the switch straight away.

True, your husband will need more than the lightish supper with which you will make do, but if you plan the family luncheon and his evening meal in one, as suggested in Chapter XII, Method in the Kitchen (pp. 104–5), there won't be much more to do than to cook fresh vegetables. Don't scamp this! Vegetables, in plenty, are so important to health, and restaurants rarely supply adequate portions. Cut out the frills, but make it a point of honour that both of you have one good, square home-cooked meal each day. There may not be much in the meat line, but you can see to it that the veg. are there.

Of course, vegetables take time to prepare, so you'll probably have to cut out pies and other pastry, except perhaps at the weekend occasionally. Those pretty little cold sweets, jellies, creams and the like, that look so attractive and take a whole afternoon to produce, will have to go, too. Confine yourself to fruit—raw, stewed or canned—for dessert. When there is milk to spare, a custard or milky pudding will add to the nourishment without much trouble. Every so often it may be possible to buy a good tart or flan ready-made at the cake shop or baker's. In the winter, simple boiled puddings, if liked, don't take long. And as a treat, a savoury can dress up the repast sometimes, provided it's not too exacting in the preparation.

A pity to bring down your exciting little dinners for two to a utilitarian nursery level? Perhaps, but better that than you should get 'nervy' and overdone. When planning the meals, don't despise a cold supper periodically. Preceded by a good soup it can be enjoyable as well as nourishing, and it will give you breathing space between putting baby to bed and the next job. When shopping, too, keep your eyes open for any canned meals. Sometimes they're heavy on 'points', but in your present circumstances they have a good deal in their favour.

If cake-making does not have to be given up temporarily, concentrate on quick, fool-proof recipes (Chapter XIII, pp. 112–13, for suggestions) and make full use of any good partly-prepared mixtures. There is an excellent make of sweetened sponge sandwich mixture on the market that needs the addition of eggs only. It doesn't require lengthy beating, either. The new Danish 'sweephat' which comes to the shops now and then, is a time-saver, and good too. It contains egg, milk, sugar and vegetable fat, so that a certain amount of measuring out and preliminaries are made unnecessary. At 2*s.* 6*d.* a lb. it seems expensive, but the quality, and its simplicity in use, make it worth buying occasionally.

Weekly Cleaning must certainly be cut down. It won't affect the comfort of the home if surrounds are polished much less often and furniture left to itself save for an occasional rub up with the duster. When you get physically stronger and no longer worried by your new responsibilities, you will be able to manage a little more housework, but take it easily!

Get into the habit of anticipating work as far as possible. The Dutch have a proverb: "Any woman can clean a house; it takes a wise woman to keep it clean." So always take a look round before going out of a room, in case there is anything to be taken with you. Try to think ahead and co-ordinate two jobs. For instance, if you take a damp cloth with you when dusting you can remove any noticeable marks on the paint, and so dispense with paint-cleaning proper for quite a while. Give new methods a trial too. If you give the spoons and forks a boil, as described in Chapter VIII, p. 74, once a month, the tarnish will be kept at bay without ordinary plate cleaning.

Bathroom and kitchen floors do need regular attention. If you find the on-hands-and-knees polishing rather exhausting, perhaps you could get once-weekly help for these jobs? Discuss it with your husband; he may volunteer to do it himself. It's a task men usually do more efficiently than women anyway, though they tend to be heavy-handed on the polish. Your husband may well take on the vacuuming at weekends too, thus relieving you of one further cleaning chore.

Washing will be increased enormously, so pare down on the time devoted to laundering household and personal things. Those frilly net curtains could stay up a couple of weeks longer without lowering your standards greatly, or maybe it would be better to have simpler ones, or none at all, for a while? Table mats can be just washed through, not starched. A rather higher laundry bill, for your husband's shirts, say, may be a justifiable extravagance. Otherwise, what about investing in a washing machine? There is such a thing as hire-purchase, remember.

Ironing *can* prove a severe strain. Don't let it. Train yourself to sit down while working, as suggested in Chapter XIV, Doing the Washing. Follow the advice given there (pp. 129–30) on minimising the work. Even if you have always pressed your husband's underwear, try putting it through the wringer only. Ten to one he won't even notice. Woollies don't need ironing, either, and many things besides. Ration yourself with light blouses, for instance, perhaps wearing an Aertex shirt in the house instead. And even if you're sick of wearing a smock, remember how it saves your clothes! You can go back to those saucy little aprons, in which you look so gay, later on, when there's less washing to be done.

HOW TO PLAN YOUR DAY.

Even when all these adjustments have been made, you'll still be doing two jobs instead of one, and the second, that of being a mother, will loom all-important. So arrange your order of work to suit your new life. You will have to evolve your own routine. Every baby is an individual. No two, nor their mothers, are quite alike; and what answers beautifully with Mrs. A. down the road won't suit *your* young man at all. A word of warning, too, before we go on to a typical order of work that you can take as a starting point. Babies are very punctual, and hate to be kept waiting. So once you've worked out a satisfactory time-table, do stick to it. Babies also detest changes and surprises, and say so, loudly and clearly. So both of you will be far happier if you cut out anything that interferes with the normal proceedings. A day's outing with a cross baby, even to visit doting grandparents, becomes a day's misery. Worse still, it may be days before you can get him back to your happy little routine again.

Suppose baby has his first feed of the day at 6 a.m. You'll probably give it to him while in bed yourself. If possible, follow the doctor's advice and have a quarter of an hour's further relaxation in bed before getting up. Then go to it with a will, for from then on until 9.30 a.m., when bathing baby must begin, there's a lot to be done!

As soon as breakfast is over, start on the washing. It helps, of course, to put nappies to soak in cold water as soon as discarded. Keep wet and soiled ones separate. The former need warm water only; the latter a pure soap or soap flakes such as Lux, without soda. Ideally, give all a boil every day, again using pure soap. Rinse very well. Then get on to the line, preferably out of doors, as quickly as possible.

Woollies can go into a basin of warm soap-substitute lather. If left immersed while the napkins are dealt with, they'll need squeezing out and rinsing only. Treat other baby-clothes and bed linen in the ordinary way, soaking any stained or wet articles in cold water first. If you're rushed, it may be easier to put to soak in the morning, and to wash through later.

While nappies are boiling, try to do the breakfast dishes, and perhaps the bathroom and any other wet jobs. If you can get the beds made, too, you're a smart worker!

Have everything ready for the bath, so that you can get it over expeditiously before a hungry baby is crying for sustenance. In whatever room you do the bathing, have a corner dedicated to the bath kit, and keep it together: clothes-horse, bath, basket, towels and your flannel and mackintosh aprons. Then out comes the whole lot when you're ready to start. It saves time wondering "Have I got everything?" and prevents the nerve-racking experience of having baby in the bath before you realise you've left the towel, or something equally vital, out of reach.

Bath and dressing safely over, there's the feed. Then into his cot with him, or the pram out of doors if the weather is fine, for a nap. You will be fortunate to finish much before 11 a.m.

After all this, you'll probably feel in need of a cup of coffee or something yourself. While sipping it, run over in your mind the rest of the day's programme, and decide what must be done, what you can let slide. Then on again! With any luck, baby shouldn't need much attention before his next feed at 2 p.m., though it's unwise to depend upon complete peace.

So you have roughly two hours, before your own lunch, for cooking, housework or any family washing. Some days a 'run over' the rooms will have to content you. On others you can, perhaps, plan a cold supper and do one of the rooms, or tackle some washing. But so long as the place is clean enough not to affront you, don't worry about the detail. As we've said before, better floor surrounds or furniture in need of polish, or mirrors a little dull, than an over-tired wife and mother, or insufficiently nourishing meals.

In fact, before you begin any cleaning, it's a good idea to get the midday vegetables prepared. Otherwise there might be the temptation to go without, or skimp them, when you see the time flying on. Ideally, of course, vegetables should be peeled immediately before being cooked, but a sensible compromise must often be made. Put potatoes in the saucepan as soon as peeled or scraped. When you cook them, use the water with which they have been covered. Wash and roughly divide greens such as cabbage, but don't shred until the last minute.

After the 2 p.m. feed and changing, you ought to have a pause with your feet up. If you can't lie down to sleep, you can perhaps have twenty minutes or so on the couch with some mending, or the paper. As soon after 3 p.m. as possible you'll want to be ready to take baby out and to do any necessary shopping. If the weather is fine, you may follow the example of many young mothers to-day and have a cup of tea while you're out. A day too wet for baby airing may give you a chance to tackle some cleaning or make cakes, but this shouldn't happen often. In any case, your deadline must be around 5.30 p.m., as baby must be washed and changed before he starts to demand too vocally his 6 p.m. feed.

All going smoothly, 6.30 p.m. sees him safely tucked up in bed and on his way to sleep. Again barring the usual accidents, he should leave you in peace until about 10 p.m., when you feed him and put him down again for the night.

Perhaps before you begin on the supper preparations you can put soiled nappies to soak, or, in an emergency, wash out a few more. There may even be time for a little ironing. If yours is a bottle baby, there'll be an additional job, that of sterilising the bottles and teats. It's as well to have a set time for it, and unless your husband will take over the whole operation, now is as good a moment as any to get it done. Keep everything together, covered with a piece of butter muslin, in a special place, such as inside the larder.

But don't undertake too much before tackling the last-minute cooking. Both you and your husband will be needing your food. After the meal, given some willing help with the clearing away, you should be free of the kitchen between 8 and 8.30 p.m.

And is the rest of the day yours? Well, don't forget the ironing, and mending or knitting. But you can sit down for these, and with a companion to talk to, or a good programme on the radio, that last hour or so won't seem too much like work.

WHEN THE CRAWLING STAGE COMES.

Once you've got into the new routine, and are no longer worried as to baby's progress, things should go pretty smoothly. The joy of a very small baby is that, all being well, he will sleep for hours, thus leaving the mother free to get on.

Probably the worst period comes at the crawling-cum-toddling stage, when the young hopeful seems to have a genius for making a mess of everything, from walls to furniture, and never to be safe alone, except when in bed. Teething may add to the difficulties, too. The only consolation about this epoch is that it will pass, and quickly. About this time, baby will be changing over to normal meal-times, so that should help a little. While the transition from crawling to toddling is being made, do try to turn one downstairs room into a nursery, as suggested in Chapter IV, Layout of the Home, p. 30.

Put away anything that might get badly damaged, or with which baby might hurt himself. If possible, take up the existing carpet and have the floor covered with linoleum and washable rugs. If this is not practicable, try to borrow a large play-pen in which the active one will be safe while out of your sight. Then buy or make several pairs of dungarees, and use them as baby's regular day-time uniform for the time being. A good tip is to put large, stout patches on the knees to start with. Then when they're worn through, as they will be remarkably quickly, just take them off.

Above all, resign yourself to the fact that a home with one or more very young children in it, and no help, can't possibly look as spick and span as when there were adults only, or, for that matter, when baby was very small. You won't be the only new mother who, thinking her house was reasonably clean, gets a nasty shock when grubby little hands begin to leave their mark everywhere.

Almost invariably, this is rather a trying time, so don't worry if your standards have to drop even a little more. When baby is walking, things should become easier, and once again the days won't seem too impossibly short for all that has to be crammed into them. All the same, it's best to make up your mind that you will enjoy your children while they're young, rather than worry over any deficiencies in the appearance of the home. As the family grow up, and you get used to taking the work in your stride, you will be able to restore some of the little refinements of living that you enjoyed in the early days of marriage.

Until then, and it won't really happen until the children are at school and not coming home for a midday meal, concentrate on the essentials. Feeding the family well, if without frills, having as much time as possible out of doors with them and keeping yourself fresh enough to enjoy some leisure with your husband in the evening must come first.

Chapter XVIII

PART-TIME HOUSEWIFE

"MONEY for jam, I call it," says the career woman, thinking of her friend who has no outside work. "What I could do if I were at home all day, instead of having to cut myself in two and run a flat and a job."

Certainly, as the career woman rushes off each morning, the home she leaves behind seems a beautiful oasis from the day's cares and problems. If only she could stay and relax a while. Then she could do some of the things, such as tidying the linen cupboard, or making some decent cakes, or trying some fresh shops, she never has time for. Or so she thinks, as the train or bus carries her to the office.

But she misses the point! When you are at home all day, the work to be done stares you in the face, and there's no escaping it. The double-job woman is able to shut the door on one part of her life each morning. She may spare it a thought during the day, but at least she won't be constantly reproached by seeing what wants doing. A brisk 'once over' before leaving keeps a place looking surprisingly presentable when there is no one to dirty it during the day.

Having to do shopping in the lunch hour is a bit of a nuisance, but it doesn't encroach on the working time. Perhaps there's not much of a selection at the shops available, but then there are less meals to provide for.

So, though having an independent career and running your own home is exacting work, it's not perhaps as overwhelming as it looks at first. At any rate, not for a single woman. With a married couple, unless sex differences are forgotten and the work is shared fifty-fifty, the strain on the wife may well be too great. A man about the house usually makes more work than he performs! When there are children, outside help is essential, unless days are to become ceaseless toil.

So let's assume that you are a career woman with a small flat. You think you ought to be able to care for it on your own, if you use your brains as you do in the office. Right! Make your routine clean-cut, pared down to the bone. Plan so that you have time to enjoy your home as well as work in it.

THE DAILY ROUTINE.

By and large, the daily routine will have to be got through before you leave for work. Do all the tidying up overnight, not forgetting changing the water in the flowers and washing the ash-trays. Strip the bed as you get up, putting the clothes to hand in the order in which they will be replaced. Wipe round the lavatory basin and bath as soon as you have used them. Keep cloths, including one for the floor, and a cleaner, in the bathroom, ready to hand. Dust the dressing-table after you've made-up, to avoid loose powder blowing across the room.

WEEKLY CLEANING.

Split weekly cleaning between the weekend and one, or at most, two evenings a week. If you don't go to the office on

Saturday morning, concentrate on 'cleaning through' the flat. This means moving out furniture, polishing floors and giving more attention to the carpets than the daily hurried sweep allows for. The bathroom and lavatory will need more care, too. Make paintwork, mirrors, metal cleaning and furniture polishing the special work for one evening a week, portioning them out over three or four weeks. If Saturday morning is not free for housework, devote Friday evening to it.

LAUNDRY WORK.

Even when you send out bed linen, towels and table-cloths, there will be quite enough washing to tackle. To avoid 'wash day' evening being too tiring, squeeze through stockings and panties each night. They will almost do themselves if you put them in a suddsy solution while you are using the bathroom. Deal with tea-towels and dusters twice weekly. They take so much less time to do if not allowed to become too grubby. Wash them through again after the weekly house-cleaning. The day before the main wash, sort the things. Before going out next morning, leave to soak in cold water any 'dirty' whites; for example, net curtains. On returning home, put into a warm soapy lather any garments that need more than a quick squeeze, providing they are colour-fast. Begin on the washing proper immediately after clearing away the supper things.

There may be time to iron silks that don't need much drying. While the board is out, press any clothes that need attention. The rest of the ironing can be polished off later in the week.

SHOPPING.

'Make friends with the tradespeople' should be your first shopping rule. Most shop-assistants are glad to be helpful to other 'working women', providing there's a little give and take on both sides. Going for your rations at a regular time each week usually pays, so does carrying a string shopping bag in your handbag, and keeping your eyes open wherever you are. As far as possible, do your buying on the way to or from your work or in the lunch hour. The less left for the busy weekend the better.

COOKING.

Suit your own taste as regards cooking. Why get your meat ration at the weekend if you like to go to the theatre Saturday night, have a 'brunch' Sunday morning and a restaurant dinner with a friend on Sunday evening? Better by far to devote one evening a week to home cooking, and have your special roast then. The butcher will be glad to accommodate you if you tell him ahead when you would like your ration. Or you may like to have one evening when you bake, and the next when you entertain. There's a good choice of main dishes that can be prepared and part cooked one day, and heated through the next. In any case, it ought to be possible to cook enough for two days at a time, and to plan so that cooking and cleaning nights don't clash. If you work this way, a care-free evening with sewing and the radio, or time for a home beauty treatment night won't be too hard to accomplish.

Chapter XIX

ENTERTAINING WITH ENJOYMENT

'HAVING friends in' or 'throwing a party' according to your vocabulary and the kind of hospitality you like to offer, can be one of the pleasanter things in life. It can also be disappointingly hard work. No one really enjoys being entertained when the preparation has obviously tired out the hostess in advance. Yet the welcome seems to lack some warmth when no effort has been made to make the occasion something a little out of the ordinary. Single-handed, you mustn't be too ambitious, although very naturally you want your guests to feel that visiting you is a delightful event in every way.

The kind of hospitality to offer will depend upon your own temperament, as well as your pocket. If you're gregarious you'll like to have plenty of visitors, even if it means that there can't be very much in the way of refreshments. On the other hand, you may get more satisfaction from inviting one or two friends to tea, or to a little dinner-party every so often, knowing that, in a simple way, everything is perfect. So set your own style; and choose your guests to match. Then if you plan carefully, everyone, host and hostess included, should have a good time.

A LITTLE DINNER PARTY.

But whatever the usual programme, you'll want to show, once or twice at least, what you can do in the way of a sit-down evening meal. In-laws will like to see the new home, and you want to exhibit your skill as both hostess and cook. Combining these two rôles successfully is quite a test, but if your husband says afterwards: "You did *wonderfully*", everything will have been worthwhile.

The right kind of menu is half the battle. You want to have as much as possible prepared ahead, so that too much time won't be spent in the kitchen at the last minute. One hot course of three is probably enough. In any case, try not to have two consecutive hot ones, unless there is a hot-plate in the dining-room to obviate rushing out of the room in the middle of a meal. A trolley is a great help in serving, and is specially useful in that it can be loaded up with the dirty dishes after each course. Unless there is anything else to be brought in, it needn't be trundled out until the meal is finished.

If coffee is served, have it either in another room, or at least away from the table to allow time for you to make it freshly.

An equally good idea is to serve the first course away from the table, too. For instance, if the principle dish is something rather special like a roast bird, a hot pie or casserole, just precede it by icy tomato or fruit juice, or an aperitif glass of wine, accompanied by a dish of olives, gherkins or other little savoury appetisers. Have these ready in the sitting-room. When the main dish is about ready, make the gravy, if necessary, and place in the oven, and put on the green vegetable or vegetables. Then leave the kitchen and join the company. While you are drinking and enjoying the little appetisers with them, the greens will be cooking. After a quarter of an hour, you can slip out and dish up. With the cold sweet to follow already in the dining-room, with appropriate plates, you won't have any more anxiety over the meal.

Don't try out new dishes, however exciting the recipe seems. Save experiment for when you are alone. Avoid also anything that must be served at the exactly right moment if it is not to spoil. You won't be popular if you are immured in the kitchen when the guests arrive and only emerge to break into the conversation with the cry: "Come and eat *now*, else the soufflé will sink", or suddenly disappear after the first course to fry even the most delectable of pancakes. Because they can be prepared the day ahead and just heated through, casseroles and braised dishes, if well made, are a good choice. Chicken casserole may only be possible on rare occasions, but braised lamb cutlets or steak and kidney, or liver can all be delicious. An extra root vegetable braised in the oven also adds to the interest of a meal, especially when, like new carrots, it has colour appeal, too.

If you have good hot soup first, and a hot sweet to follow, a cold main dish is often a great success. Examples are a cold roast bird; or a platter of mixed sliced cold meats, including some canned ones; or American pork sausage meat in a raised crust; or a rather special fish mayonnaise. Suitable for the latter are shellfish, salmon when in season, halibut or turbot. Mayonnaise must be good, and the garnishing with anchovies, gherkin or olive, capers or pimento, done rather lavishly. New potatoes and peas in summer, and a well-chosen salad, at any time, are necessary accompaniments. Incidentally, don't forget the possibilities of a small, individual fish salad or 'cocktail' as the first course. Shellfish is best, arranged on a little crisp lettuce, with a good garnish and some tangy tomato sauce. It must be very cold and well-flavoured. Serve in a grape-fruit glass.

The four menus given at the end of the chapter will suggest lines on which to work.

A FRIENDLY SUPPER.

Although a small dinner-party is bound to be attempted occasionally, a more informal evening meal may usually accord better with both the budget and personal taste. When entertaining friends who come often, and to whose home one goes in turn, this is nearly always so. According to circumstances, and the time of the year, such a meal can be a two-course sit-down one in the dining-room, a 'fork supper' round the sitting-room fire, or even a 'house special' served in the kitchen, direct from the stove. Whatever you choose, it's best as a rule to stick largely to unrationed food, to save embarrassment on the part of the guests, and to avoid anything that requires elaborate table setting or too many dishes. Visitors of this kind usually help with the washing-up afterwards, and the more quickly it can be polished off, the more pleased will everyone be.

It's rather pleasant to get a reputation for doing one or two dishes extra well. One young couple are envied for the success of their spaghetti suppers. It means saving a couple of weeks' cheese ration, but while 'points' cheese is available, that's no great hardship. Fresh spaghetti is bought and cooked for each party, a quarter of a pound a head (uncooked) being allowed. The hostess has learnt how to make a really good sauce with onions, tomatoes, paprika, herbs and perhaps a few mushrooms. The host concentrates on an accompanying salad which he dresses at table. Italian bread sticks and rough Algerian wine give a nice touch, and home-bottled fruit with marshmallow cream and coffee make a popular finish.

When another young couple want to invite their choicest friends they announce: "Fish and chips in the kitchen after the rugger game." It means lashing out on a big bottle of frying oil, but that lasts more than once. The fillets are egg-and-breadcrumbed ahead, but the potatoes, ready-peeled, are chipped at the last moment, to avoid discoloration, by the hostess, who acts as kitchen-maid while her husband is cook. There is no waiting. Each guest is helped right from the pan. As this meal is served at high-tea time, tea is the chosen beverage, with home-made scones, cakes and jam as side dishes. The guests say it's 'super'.

There's no limit to the popular meals that can be devised for this kind of party. They can be quite inexpensive, too. The great thing is that everything should be good of its kind and served up in a manner appropriate to the menu. Some suggestions are given at the end of the chapter.

"COME TO TEA . . . OR FOR COFFEE THIS EVENING . . ."

All in all, it's the tea-party, or the evening by the fire with a tray of sandwiches and cakes brought in half-way, that's the most popular form of entertaining to-day. Here success depends largely upon the presentation. Fine napery, attractive china and, if used, softly gleaming silver, seem to make everything more delectable. All the same, learn to make good tea, put enough filling in your sandwiches, and either save up enough fats and sugar to make cakes that are really good of their kind, or patronise a shop that goes in for quality. Nothing is more disillusioning than to be given sponges that owe their colour and lightness to tinted raising agents rather than eggs, or iced cakes that taste mainly of soda bicarbonate and sawdust. A vast quantity of food is not necessary, but it should be appetising.

With only two people's rations there is not much margin, but, if you collect and try out recipes intelligently, you'll be able to choose from such things as a fatless sponge, an eggless chocolate cake, biscuits that use syrup instead of sugar, and so on, so that you are not caught out by a shortage of one ingredient that is usually considered essential.

For a small tea-party it's a good idea to use creamed margarine for the sandwiches and save the butter for a little plateful of bread and butter, cut thin and spread as liberally as possible. This is always a special favourite, particularly with older people. Indeed, with home-made jam it's a feast for the gods.

When the party is an evening one, vary the sandwiches by having some 'open' ones of the 'smorrebrod' type, using crispbread or salted biscuits for them. Hot baking-powder rolls, roughly split open and filled with either a sweet or a savoury mixture, are liked at most meals. They are very quick and economical to make and require less buttering than sandwiches.

FOR THE CHILDREN.

At a children's party, don't make the mistake of providing too many cakes, or too rich ones. A Victoria sponge mixture, baked in a square tin, cut into shapes and iced with different-coloured water-icing is probably the main favourite. To-day's children tend to prefer savouries to sweets, so sandwiches with grated cheese and celery salt or marmite disappear quickly. On the other hand, all youngsters love jellies and ice-cream at tea, especially if the former are served in fancy shapes or are attractively coloured.

And finally, to get a reputation for serving a really good cup, make tea this way. Put the tea in the warmed pot, allowing a caddyspoonful for three tea-cups and a heaped teaspoonful for two. Then add enough freshly boiling water to cover the tea to a depth of about one inch. Keep the kettle boiling over a low heat for another minute, when add a further cupful of water. Repeat until the pot is full. When pouring out, never empty the tea-pot before adding more water. In this way, the tea will be infusing all the time, making the most of the strength and the flavour, without getting 'stewed'.

FOUR MENUS FOR A SIMPLE DINNER-PARTY

1.

Shrimp or crawfish cocktail.

Chicken in casserole or braised kidneys.
Vegetables in season.

Fruit flan.

2.

Hors d'œuvres.

Hot steak and kidney pie or raised pork pie.
Vegetables in season.

Coffee cream or caramel custard.

3.

A good soup.

Cold roast poultry or platter of cold meats or crab or turbot mayonnaise with salad and potatoes.

Hot Christmas pudding or mushroom patties.

4.

Tomato or fruit juice or apéritif with cocktail savouries.

Hot roast joint or poultry with sauce or seasoning.
Vegetables in season.

Fruit salad and mock cream or hot fruit pie.

FOUR MENUS FOR AN INFORMAL EVENING MEAL

1.

Tomato juice.

Creamed white fish with fluffy potatoes and mock tartare sauce.

Hot 'cake' pudding with baked apple.

2.

Baked sausages.
Mushrooms, tomatoes.
Scalloped or jacket potatoes.

Butterscotch tart.

3.

Hearty soup.

Crispbread and baking powder rolls, with cheese and savoury fillings.

Fruit salad.

4.

Savoury spaghetti.
Bread sticks.

Green salad.

Ice-cream and fruit.
Cake.

Chapter XX

BEAUTY WHILE YOU WORK

"DON'T have dishpan hands" used to be a popular slogan in a hand-lotion advertisement. The copywriter had certainly got a good 'story', for housework and cooking can be hard on the hands. It's not that, in a modern home at least, there's so much very dirty work, but the tendency is for hands to be in and out of water, and hot water at that. This opens the pores, so that any dirt doesn't merely mark the surface, but gets worked in. At least, that's what happens if intelligent care isn't taken.

HANDS.

Back in Chapter VI, when discussing the daily routine, grouping dry and wet jobs together was suggested. It means less in and out of water for the hands. A lot of wear and tear will be saved if you follow this principle right through the day. When you have had your hands in water, for doing the dishes, say, don't just give them a half wipe on the kitchen towel before starting to dry up. Wash your hands carefully with soap and then rinse under the cold tap. *Then* dry, taking care to finish the job properly and to push back the cuticles as you do so.

Sometimes, of course, when there is a knock at the door when your hands are covered in dough or you have to run from the washtub to the stove, you'll slip up on the routine, but do try to follow it as thoroughly as possible. In American kitchens, a little fitment taking an inverted bottle of hand lotion is often fixed over the sink. It is so convenient that you get into the way of using it, after washing-up, say, quite automatically. We may not have such gadgets, but there's plenty of lotion about, and a bottle lasts quite a long while. Keep it in the kitchen, and use it while on the job, for best results!

A simple tin of Vaseline is another hand-saver. Rub a thin coating over your hands if you're going to plunge them into very hot water. It is protective. Rubber gloves are useful, too. Some people like these very much, others find them clumsy. You must experiment for yourself; but for jobs such as cleaning the lavatory, or the gas oven if you've let it get neglected, or even for washing over the floor, they're well worth while. Use them too, to protect your hands while using a strong bleach, or a poison. If you don't like gloves, there is a new cream on the market that is rubbed into the hands before any dirty wet task is undertaken. It is claimed that its use prevents dirt sinking in. A companion cream is designed for dirty dry jobs.

Vegetable cleaning can mark the fingers very badly. Here again, some people like to wear rubber gloves. Otherwise, scrub the mud from vegetables with a brush before scraping or peeling. Afterwards, rub the stained fingers with pumice stone, before giving them a normal wash.

For dusty jobs, such as cleaning out the fireplace or boiler, or grimy ones like metal cleaning, it's best to wear an old pair of leather gloves. Even for dusting, gloves are a useful protection. Housemaid's cotton gloves are now obtainable. These must be washed out as frequently as your duster.

HAIR.

Next to the hands, the hair is a sufferer—or more exactly, it gets pretty grubby unless it is always wrapped up when any dust-raising job is in process. Use a scarf, cap or a clean duster pinned like a nurse's square over head and hair when doing the rooms, and especially while the vacuum cleaner is being emptied or the mop shaken out. Brush your hair thoroughly each night and wash the hairbrush frequently. Then with a shampoo every ten days or so, all will be well.

SKIN.

If you've been doing office work before you started as a full-time housewife the chances are that your skin will improve, rather than the reverse, in your new rôle. You'll miss the big-city grime and soot which are so injurious to the skin, and will probably find you need less make-up, or a much lighter one. If you're going shopping when there's a nice fine rain coming down, it will pay to leave off all cosmetics except lipstick, so that your complexion gets a beauty bath. It's a good idea to give your face a treatment on wash-day, too. Cleanse your skin before you begin, then apply nourishing cream. The steam will soften it so that it is readily absorbed by the pores. When you've finished the washing, take off the surplus cream with cotton wool or tissue and finish with cleansing milk or a mild astringent before making up. Give your hands a little care at the same time. It's thoughtful to file nails, if necessary, before the laundry work begins, and to rub a little oil in the cuticles. Afterwards, go round the cuticles with an orange stick; they will 'shape up' beautifully.

Then carefully massage some nourishing hand cream into the back of the hands and round the nail base. Again, take off any oily excess with cotton wool.

FIGURE.

What about the figure? Some women will always let themselves go, just as others will take thought about posture, but on the whole, housework is far better for one than a sitting-down job. There's less chance of the spreading round the middle that dogs those who do clerical work. On the other hand, it's easy to get tired from standing too much, especially if you're unused to it. The remedy for this is to make full use of the kitchen stool and to wear comfortable shoes.

For the rest, it's largely a question of using your common sense. Your tummy muscles will be contracted if you make a round back when using a dustpan and brush, but when you bend from the knees and go down to a squatting posture, it's as good as an abdominal exercise from the daily dozen. Sweeping can be good too, also reaching up for dusting, while if you arrange your shopping and other excursions so that you get a really good walk each day, your health, and so your looks, will benefit.

Chapter XXI

A MAN ABOUT THE HOUSE

THROUGHOUT this book we've assumed that though the housewife has no paid outside help, her husband will 'give a hand' with various jobs. Once upon a time such an assumption would have been strange indeed. To-day it is accepted in almost all homes, and certainly in middle-class ones, that the bread-winner who is out all day does have certain obligations of this kind. How matter of fact this has become was illustrated by a recent advertisement in the personal column of *The Times*. Two young Naval officers, wanting accommodation as paying guests near their station, offered as a recommendation their qualification of being 'good washers-up'.

Yet, in spite of all this, there's little doubt that this sharing of the chores does occasion a good deal of heart-burning. The reason is mainly to be found in the different attitude of men and women to the subject. The single-handed housewife has a big job, and one that can seldom be compressed into an eight-hour working day. To do it well, and not get over-tired in the process, she must have some co-operation from the other members of the family. She sees this only too clearly, and expects that co-operation as a right.

Her husband is usually ready to admit the justice of her claim, but deep down in his heart there's a very strong feeling, handed down through generations of masculine mastership, that the home is his wife's concern. He'll help, of course, but as a generous concession, not as a right.

If at the very beginning you and your husband can face and reconcile these two opposing viewpoints, the outlook will be good. It takes some give and take, naturally, but that's an ingredient necessary in every working agreement, not only in home-making!

On your side, do remember that your husband's work has its strains and stresses too, not the least of them being rush-hour travelling. When he gets in, let him rest and relax, with a drink, or tea. Then, when he has changed and feels refreshed, have dinner ready without any waiting, even though it has meant some sacrifice on your part to keep to the time-table. He'll help clear away afterwards with a much better grace because of your understanding when he came in.

A routine is good, but be generous, too. If he's had an exceptionally trying day offer to do the washing-up, say. Then when you feel off-colour, he'll be more likely to notice and suggest that he takes on some of your duties.

Treat 'nights off' in the same manner. When his men friends come in for a bridge four, be the hostess at dinner but the kitchen maid afterwards as well. In return, when you have a feminine party, he'll rally round so that you can feel pampered for a change.

Just how much your husband can be expected to contribute 'in kind' to running the home depends upon his work, how exacting it is, and upon your individual temperaments and circumstances. If he has a long journey, so that he has to leave early and return late, it would be unfair to expect as much as if he had a shorter working day. At times of stress, on the other hand, as when baby comes, the average husband will be ready to put in perhaps more than his share. Many a young father is happy to take his turn at bathing baby so that his wife may have a little respite, or be able to get ahead with the evening meal.

In many households, husbands take on certain definite tasks: doing the boiler and the coal perhaps, every morning, and the washing-up every evening. At weekends they will add the vegetables and the sitting-room fire to their share, or perhaps be the one to get up first and take up breakfast to the feminine member of the partnership.

But every married couple must make their own rules. Perhaps your husband rather likes cooking. Well, let him take over at weekends. You can become housemaid and washer-up too, if that makes for greater harmony. If he prefers to leave you to control the cuisine, you may find he will quite happily run the vacuum cleaner over the rooms on Sunday morning, and wield the duster too, thus giving you a rest from the usual routine.

When children get old enough, and at five years old they are eager to help, even if their attempts are not very practical, let them take a share. Don't differentiate between boys and girls. Both should learn how to cook a simple meal, and to clear it away, before the teens are reached. Although grumbles are natural, no youngster was ever any the worse for doing a share of the household chores. In fact, it's noticeable that in the happiest families, everyone 'pitches in' even if it is, very rightly, Mother who does the lion's part and keeps the whole machine running sweetly.

CONCLUSION

To show the way to run one's home without help, efficiently and happily too, has been the object of this book. But a guide can only point out the path. Of course there will be rough places on the way, and setbacks. Days when the jelly won't jell, the housework seems a meaningless grind, and even the visit to the shops nothing but a drag. Other times, though, the sun will shine, everything will go like clockwork, and you'll feel that nothing in the world can be half so satisfying as running your own home the way you do.

So don't despair if at first everything doesn't go exactly to plan. Practice makes perfect, and once you've grasped the general principles you'll soon work out a routine to suit your personality and circumstances.

As the mechanics of running a home become familiar, you'll discover how much else there is to the job. Because you're always learning, it will never get stale. The joy of creative work, exhausting though it can be, is that it enriches the personality. Running a home may seem unspectacular and ordinary, but making a success of it, so that the home is a happy one for all who live in it, is creative work to rank with the best.

Appendix I

EQUIPMENT

The following is offered merely as a guide to the kind of thing obtainable. It does not set out to be in any way complete. Although an attempt has been made to give a *representative* selection, neither the inclusion nor the omission of any makes or models must be taken as a recommendation or otherwise of their quality or performance.

WATER HEATERS.

1. Solid-fuel Boilers.

These are normally only suitable for installation by house-owners. Many people think of a solid fuel boiler as being dirty and rather erratic in performance, though cheap to run. The modern closed-fire continuous-burning domestic boilers, with magazine or gravity feed, have largely overcome the disadvantages of the older, more familiar open-fire types. They do give *constant* hot water in generous quantity and need little attention. Fuelling once in twenty-four hours only is usual. Fire grates are designed for easy cleaning. Removal of ash or clinker can be done without letting the fire out. Riddling of the ashes from the fire is not needed more often than twice in the twenty-four hours, while the ash-pan needs emptying only once. The boilers have a streamlined, attractive appearance, with enamelled surfaces that only need wiping over with a damp cloth to keep clean. Radiators can be run off many models, thus giving background heating in several rooms as well as providing the hot-water supply. All this is done at a lower cost for fuel than by any other type of water heater.

Against this must be placed the rather heavy initial outlay. The prices quoted below are for boilers only. The hot-water tank or cistern is not included, and fitting costs may be appreciable. It is sometimes difficult to compare boilers because the technical terms used to describe them are unfamiliar. The rating in British thermal units gives some idea of comparative performance. Advice from a heating engineer is suggested. Different makes are more easily obtainable in various parts of the country. Also, some boiler fuels have a better distribution in some localities than in others.

(*a*) IDEAL NO. O-M MAGAZINE BOILER provides enough constant hot water for the average small family, i.e. serves 20-gallon cylinder, and will also heat small radiators (60 sq. ft. of heating surface) as well. If used solely for hot water, will service a 40-gallon tank or cylinder. Burns ½–1¼ in. coke or anthracite nuts. Approximate size: 39 in. high overall, 19 in. wide, 21 in. deep. Cream stove-enamelled front; black vitreous-enamelled iron platework. Approximate price £18. (Ideal Boilers and Radiators, Ltd., Ideal House, Great Marlborough Street, London, W.1.)

(*b*) THE 'BARWISE' MAGAZINE BOILER, MODEL 50, is designed for a very generous supply of constant hot water. Will serve systems with storage cylinders from 35–80 gallons capacity. If a 30–35-gallon indirect cylinder is installed, will serve small radiators, too. Rating: 50,000 B.T.U. per hour. Burns small coke or anthracite nuts ¾–1 in. size. Approximate size: 40 in. high overall, 21½ in. wide, 27 in. deep. Cream vitreous-enamelled front, black vitreous enamel top. Price £21. (Barwise (Engineers), Ltd., Waller Street Works, Carlisle.)

(*c*) THE 'WATTS' AUTOMATIC GRAVITY-FEED BOILER provides constant hot water and heats radiators for a house of the 4–5-bedroom size. A small thermostatically-controlled electrically-driven fan is incorporated in the boiler to keep the fire at the correct burning rate. Rating: 60,000 B.T.U. per hour.

Burns anthracite grains or peas. Size: 41 in. high, 17 in. wide, 19 in. deep. Overall finish, heat-resisting enamel, with top cover, fire-door and ash-tray in black. Price £67 10*s*. (Brockhouse Heater Co., Ltd., Victoria Works, Hill Top, West Bromwich.)

(*d*) 'AUTO-ANTHRA' GRAVITY-FEED AUTOMATIC BOILER is another model with electrically-driven fan, designed to provide background heating and constant hot water for the family-sized house. Burns anthracite grains. Model AA1: Rating 40,000 B.T.U. per hour. Approximate size: 39 in. high overall, 18 in. wide, 16½ in. deep. Price £62 10*s*. Model AA2: Rating 60,000 B.T.U. per hour is slightly higher and wider. Price £75. Both models finished in cream, green or blue stove enamel, with black, green or blue vitreous-enamel doors and top. (Hartley & Sugden Ltd., White Rose Boiler Works, Halifax.)

2. GAS WATER HEATERS.

These are mainly suitable for installation by house owners, although often a suitable appliance can be obtained on hire purchase, or may even be rented from the local gas company. The fitting costs may be substantial if long lengths of pipe have to be run, or taps have to be put in odd positions. The small sink heaters are a possible exception as they do not need flues, and usually require only a short length of piping. With a suitable installation, performance is excellent and trouble-free. Running costs of gas water heaters tend to be, on the average, higher than for solid fuel ones, but no work is involved. There are three main types of gas water heaters. Which will prove most suitable depends on the kind of use and amount of hot water required. Local gas-supply show-rooms can give helpful advice. Prices given do *not* include the cost of fitting, or of a separate cylinder, if the latter is necessary.

(*a*) THE CIRCULATOR, which supplies hot water to a cylinder or tank which is normally the storage tank of a solid-fuel hot-water system. A circulator can be fitted to take the place of an existing solid-fuel boiler, or be used in conjunction with it. For example, in winter the solid-fuel boiler would be lit, while in summer the gas circulator takes its place. The gas can also 'step up' the solid-fuel boiler if extra hot water is required quickly. The circulator gives almost unlimited hot water and is a good choice for the family house. A flue must be fitted.

The 'Emperor' Circulator, in vitreous enamel, cream or mottled grey, with automatic heat regulation and safety cut-off device. No. 1 for 25–30-gallon-size storage tank. Approximate size: 32 in. high, 13 in. wide, 21 in. deep. Price £27, plus purchase tax. Without cut-off device £22 10*s*., plus purchase tax. Also larger sizes. (Thomas Potterton & Sons, Ltd., 20–30 Buckhold Road, London, S.W.18.)

(Wall-fixing models, made by Richmond's Gas Stove Co., and Mains Water Heaters, also obtainable.)

(*b*) THE STORAGE HEATER is similar in principle to the circulator, but no separate cylinder is required, as the storage tank is an integral part of the appliance. This results in reduced running costs, as the shape and the insulation of the tank is of the most effective design for the purpose. A storage heater can be run intermittently or continuously, and supplies plentiful hot water to basins, baths and sink. It is entirely automatic in action. When the whole of the water in the cylinder is hot, the gas lowers itself to the very small flame required to keep the water hot. The storage heater normally requires a flue.

The 'Equator' Storage Water Heater No. 153. White-painted finish. 12 gallons capacity. Overall size: 52 in. high, 22 in. wide, 16½ in. deep. Price £28 15*s*., plus purchase tax. No. 157, 18 gallons capacity, is rather wider and deeper but a trifle shorter. £33 10*s*. 6*d*., plus purchase tax. (Richmond's Gas Stove Co., Ltd., Grapplehall Works, Warrington.)

(A sink storage heater is also made.)

(*c*) THE INSTANTANEOUS WATER HEATER heats water as required. This type has the advantage of being relatively small and compact, and can often be 'built in' with other fixtures. There are three main styles: for supply to the sink; the bath only, and to sink; bath and basin.

*The 'Ascot' Gas Sink Water Heater R.*12 supplies 1 gallon, raised through 40° F. per minute, or ½ gallon, raised 80° F. per minute. It can be fixed in place of the cold-water tap. White vitreous-enamel finish. No flue is necessary. Size: 25 in. high, 6½ in. diameter. Price £6 18*s*., plus purchase tax.

The 'Ascot' Instantaneous Gas Boiling-Water Heater RS 52/1 is an improved sink heater which supplies boiling, hot or warm water according to the setting of the hot tap. Boiling water flows at the rate of 2–3 pints per minute, and proportionately more hot or warm water, according to the temperature. No flue is normally required. White vitreous-enamel finish. Size: 29½ in. high, 7 in. diameter. Price £11 15*s*., plus purchase tax.

*The 'Ascot' S.G.*32/1 *Single Point Water Heater* supplies hot water at the approximate rate of 4¼ gallons per minute raised through 40° F., or 2 gallons per minute raised through 65° F. Flue and ventilation in bathroom required. White vitreous-enamel finish. Size: 42 in. high, 15 in. wide, 8 in. deep. Price £13 17*s*. 6*d*., plus purchase tax. (Ascot Gas Water Heaters, Ltd., 43 Park Street, London, W.1.)

The De la Rue Type DLR 175 *Instantaneous Heater* supplies hot water to bath, basin and sink. Approximate rate of flow, 3½ gallons per minute raised through 40° F., or rather more than 2 gallons raised through 65° F. Green or cream plastic-finished outer casing with contrasting 'louvres' over the built-in draught diverter. Flue required. Approximate size: 36 in. high, 16 in. wide, 11 in. deep. Price £20, plus purchase tax. (De la Rue Gas Development, Ltd., Imperial House, 34/36 Regent Street, London, W.1.)

3. Electric Water Heaters.

One main type, the storage water heater, is admirably suited for installation by the tenant in a flat or house. As these heaters are self-contained and do not require separate tanks or flues, fixing is comparatively simple and inexpensive. In most districts, the local Electricity Board showrooms will have models on hire-purchase terms, and possibly for hire, as well as for sale. These appliances are easily removable and do *not* become landlord's fixtures.

Another type, comprising immersion heaters and circulators, is designed for use in conjunction with solid-fuel heaters for supplying hot water when the main boiler is not lit. These often cost rather more to fit, and may become landlord's fixtures unless an arrangement is made at the time of installation. With all electric types, the hot-water supply is completely automatic and dependable. No work is involved at all. Generally speaking, initial costs, including fitting, of electric water-heating equipment are lower than for appliances using solid fuel. To balance this, running costs tend to be appreciably higher. But when a comparatively small amount of hot water is required, the much lower running costs of solid fuel may not prove any more economical in the end. Compared with gas, the costs of fitting and using electric water heaters are roughly the same, though much depends on respective local charges.

(*a*) the storage water heater.

The 'Sadia' Sink Water Heater (wall model type). Thermostatically controlled. 1½ or 3 gallons of piping-hot water (according to size), available within half to three quarters of an hour. When the current is left on the water is swiftly reheated as drawn off. White vitreous-enamel finish. 3 gallons capacity approximately £11, plus purchase tax. Approximate cost of fitting £3–£5. Easily removed by undoing four fixing screws, one water connection, and disconnecting electricity. (Aidas Electric Works, Ltd., Sadia Works, Rowdell Road, Northolt, Middlesex.)

The 'Charlton Twin' (two-in-one free-standing model to supply all taps). Thermostatically controlled. Entirely automatic action. Supplies plentiful 'constant hot water' to sink, basin and bath. 'Recovery rate', full on, 1 hour. Can be used intermittently if desired. 20-gallon capacity. White vitreous-enamel finish. Price £21, plus purchase tax. A 15-gallons-capacity model is designed but not yet in production. (Johnson & Phillips, Ltd., Columbia House, Aldwych, London, W.C.2.)

Cost of fitting to existing installation depends upon conditions on site; say £7–£12 if no extensive alteration or new cistern is necessary. Removable by unscrewing two water connections and disconnecting electricity.

(*b*) THE IMMERSION HEATER is designed for installation in an existing tank or cylinder. It provides an auxiliary method of heating to a solid-fuel boiler. The immersion heater is most efficient when left switched on continuously, but under thermostatic control, to provide constant hot water. The tank or cylinder must be lagged or heat-insulated by at least 2½ in. of granulated cork or glass fibre. Not every domestic water installation is capable of being adapted satisfactorily to electric heating. Sometimes extensive pipe alterations may be necessary. Sound technical advice is essential, otherwise the working may be unsatisfactory and running costs high.

The 'Hotpoint'. 3 kw. size (12 gallons at 140° F. per hour) approximately £7, plus purchase tax. 2 and 1 kw. sizes, approximately £6 and £5 respectively, plus purchase tax. (Hotpoint Electrical Appliance Co., Ltd., Crown House, Aldwych, London, W.C.2.)

(*c*) THE ELECTRIC CIRCULATOR, like the immersion heater, is installed in an existing tank or cylinder for auxiliary heating, but is suitable for *soft-water districts* only. This appliance, also thermostatically controlled, is suitable for intermittent hot water, say for baths only, as a small quantity of hot water is available soon after switching on. Lagging is not so vitally necessary as when hot water at any time is required, but is desirable. A removable jacket can be used instead of the cork or glass wool insulation.

The 'Santon' Circ-Stat No. 328. 3 kw. size (12 gallons at 140° F. per hour), approximately £9, plus purchase tax. 2 kw. size, approximately £9, plus purchase tax. (Santon Ltd., Somerton Works, Newport, Mon.)

The cost of fitting for both immersion heaters and circulators depends on the amount of pipe alteration, and whether a new cylinder is necessary. Assuming that *no* pipe alteration or cylinder is required, approximately £8–£10 with lagging, £5–£7 without. To remove, the heater is unscrewed bodily, after disconnection of electricity. Normally, these heaters are considered as landlord's fixtures, but most landlords are satisfied if the heater is replaced by a screwed plug, so that the installation can continue to be heated by solid fuel as before.

Note: The performance of a water heater of any type largely depends upon the efficiency of the *installation*. A well-lagged tank or cylinder and the correct arrangement of piping to avoid heat-loss make all the difference to the supply, and to the running costs. When considering fitting, or altering, a hot-water system it pays to take qualified technical advice.

SPACE HEATERS.

1. SOLID-FUEL GRATES.

There has been an enormous improvement in these since before the war. The modern open fire has all the old-time cheerful appearance but, as well, gives out more heat for the fuel burned, and is much less dirty, smoky and work-making.

(*a*) THE CONTINUOUS-BURNING OPEN FIRE is one of the most attractive types. Once lit it can be kept in all the winter if liked. At night, a hood or lid turns the open fire into a slow-combustion one, burning very little fuel, yet keeping the room at comfortable warmth. There are many good makes. Most, though supplied in sizes to fit standard grate openings, need some builder's work to fix. Some can be simply pushed into position, as for example the

J.L.C. Continuous-Burning Open Coal Fire. This will fit into most existing fireplaces and does *not* become a landlord's fixture. It burns ordinary house coal and can be an open fire during the day, a closed fire at night. Ash is removed once daily, but there is no clearing out in the usual sense. In black, cream and brown mottle vitreous enamel. To fit standard 16-in. fireplace. Price £9 15*s*. (J.L.C. Fires, Ltd., 226 Abbey House, 2 Victoria Street, London, S.W.1.)

(*b*) THE CONVECTOR FIRE makes use of heat, usually lost through the surrounding brickwork, to warm the currents of air which are circulated round the back and sides of the grate. This warm air can be let into the room, or, if ducts are installed, carried to an adjoining room or upstairs bedroom. Generally speaking, these grates need installing by a builder, but the amount of fixing necessary varies. Some have a back boiler fitted for domestic hot-water supply. An interesting example is the

'Camelon' Convector Fire with Under-floor Air Control. The special feature here is that the ash is only cleared out once or twice weekly, with consequent saving of work. All the other good points of continuous-burning convector heat, lack of smoke and economy in fuel consumption, are embodied, too. The under-floor air control also means less room draughts.

A back boiler to supply a 30-gallon hot-water cylinder can be fitted. Burns all solid fuel, including coke and anthracite. Finished in vitreous enamel to match tile surround. Price £10 10*s.* upwards. Boiler from £5 10*s.* extra. (Camelon Iron Co., Ltd., Falkirk.)

(*c*) THE SMOKELESS FUEL OPEN FIRE is an effective, inexpensive type, a good choice when continuous burning is not required. Accurate air control regulates the rate of burning, so that the fire can be shut down to burn for 6–7 hours without attention. These fires burn coke, anthracite, or even ordinary coal. The gas ignition abolishes the need for laying with wood and paper. The coke used makes little dust or smoke. Most kinds can be fitted into existing fireplaces.

The 'Fulham' Grate. Made in three sizes for 14-in., 16-in. and 18-in. fire openings. 16-in. size in black vitreous enamel, price £4 10*s.* In brown or stone, £5 0*s.* 6*d.* (Eagle Range & Grate Co., Ltd., Aston, Birmingham, 6.)

(*d*) THE OPEN-CLOSE STOVE is the most economical in fuel consumption of all. It can be free-standing, in which case it is simple to remove when a tenant leaves, or built in. The inset types can be fitted to supply convection air heating to a bedroom, but the free-standing stove gives the maximum heating for a single room. Either kind can be fitted with a back boiler to supply a tank for domestic hot water or one or two small radiators.

The 'Sun-ray' Stove. Suitable for a room 20 ft. by 15 ft. by 10 ft. The free-standing model is 27 in. high, 19 in. wide and 17 in. deep. Flue outlet at back. Finished black, brown or green vitreous enamel £11 10*s.* Boiler, not including cylinder, £3 10*s.* 6*d.* extra. (Camelon Iron Co., Ltd., Falkirk.)

2. GAS FIRES.

The post-war fire doesn't look very different from older types except the radiants are simpler in shape. On the whole it gives out more heat for the amount of gas burned, and the whole fire has a longer life without any attention. Most designs are meant for intermittent use, but there are convectors and radiators in various sizes which give continuous or background heating. Portable models have returned to the market after the war-time absence. These, like the radiators, do not need the usual flue. The following are representative of the four main kinds.

(*a*) THE STANDARD FIRE, 9-radiant size, for a large room. Size: 24 in. high, 18 in. wide, 9¼ in. deep. Requires flue. In a large number of gold and silver 'clouded' colours. Price £10 2*s*. 6*d*., plus purchase tax. (Gas Light & Coke Co., 30 Kensington Church Street, London, W.8.)

For a smaller room, the CANNON INCLINED GAS FIRE K.5, 5-radiant size: 24 in. high, 14¼ in. wide. Coin bronze or matt gold finish. Price about £5, plus purchase tax. (Cannon Iron Foundries, Ltd., Deepfield, Bilston, Staffs.)

(*b*) THE 'SILENT BEAM' PANEL GAS FIRE. A new type designed to be built in, thus taking up the least possible room. A good choice for bedroom or dining-room. Silent in use, three-position tap for easy heat regulation. Requires flue. 'New World' Silent Beam No. 7505. Size: 22 in. high, 16 in. wide, 6 in. deep. In hammered-brass finish. Price £4 15*s*., plus purchase tax. (Gas Light & Coke Co., 30 Kensington Church Street, London, W.8.)

The above prices do not include fixing charges, which vary according to length of pipe to be run.

(*c*) THE PORTABLE GAS FIRE. Used with flexible tubing, this type can be 'plugged in' to any suitable connection. Economical in use and pleasing in appearance. *The 'Fa-neat' Portable Gas Fire F.A/3*, in chromium plating and cream paint. Size: 20 in. high, 12½ in. wide, 8 in. deep. Price £3 8*s*. 6*d*., plus purchase tax. A bowl type, for when a very small fire only is required, the '*Warmglow' heater*, with polished copper bowl and black base, £1 7*s*. 6*d*. and 15*s*. 6*d*. each, plus purchase tax. (Gas Light & Coke Co., 30 Kensington Church Street, London, W.8.)

(*d*) THE RADIATOR OR CONVECTOR HEATER is flueless and heats by giving out warm air. A variety of types and sizes for rooms both large and small, and corridors or halls.

The 'E.P.' Convector, Type A, in coin bronze paint. Approximate size: 30 in. high, 14 in. wide, 9 in. deep. Price £5 9*s*. 6*d*., plus purchase tax. Fitting charge not included. (Gas Light & Coke Co., 30 Kensington Church Street, London, W.8.)

Note: Similar models obtainable from most gas supply company showrooms.

3. ELECTRIC FIRES.

Here again there is no startling difference in appearance from the familiar pre-war types, but the general trend is towards greater efficiency of performance where possible. In addition to the well-known electric fires for intermittent use, there are convectors, or air warmers, and tubular heaters for background heating. Electricity Board showrooms all over the country now have good representative selections. Simple models of good make come into the following price ranges:

(*a*) FIRES (known to the trade as radiators).

Fire-bar type:
1-kw. size, price £1 10*s*.
2-kw. size, price £2 10*s*., both plus purchase tax.

Reflector type:
1-kw. size, price £1 16*s*.
2-kw. size, price £3, both plus purchase tax.

(*b*) CONVECTORS OR AIR WARMERS.

Free-standing model:
1-kw. size, price £6 6*s*.
2-kw. size, price £8, both plus purchase tax.

Steel radiator, liquid-filled type:
1-kw. size, price £10.
2-kw. size, price £14, both plus purchase tax.

(*c*) TUBULAR HEATERS. These are designed for fixing to the walls or skirting to give additional heat, or for continuous background heating. When installed with thermostatic control, they give electric 'central heating'. Rated at 60 watts per foot length, 5*s*. to 8*s*. per foot, plus purchase tax, depending on length of individual tubes.

COOKING STOVES.

1. Solid Fuel.

As with water heating by an independent boiler, the initial costs of a solid-fuel appliance tend to be comparatively high, although some reliable types of continuous-burning insulated cookers cost no more than good gas or electric ones. To balance this, the solid fuel stove is economical to run. Also, most of the new types heat water efficiently too, so that normally a separate boiler is not necessary. When a good deal of cooking has to be done, the continuous-burning, vitreous-enamelled, modern, solid-fuel stove has a lot in its favour. For the small household, or when time is more valuable than money (for even the best solid-fuel appliances need some flue cleaning, ash removal and refuelling), gas or electric cooking, when possible, is probably to be preferred. There are three main kinds of modern solid-fuel cooker.

(*a*) THE HEAT-STORAGE COOKER. This burns smokeless fuel and is heavily insulated to prevent the heat escaping. It is built with specially heavy castings, in which the heat is accumulated for use when cooking is required. The hot-plates and ovens are therefore always at cooking temperature. Ovens are thermostatically controlled. Fuel consumption is very low. This is the most expensive type to begin with, but is extremely efficient. Being free-standing, these cookers can be dismantled from a rented house and re-erected in the new premises when the tenant moves.

The Esse 'Fairy' Heat-storage Cooker No. 3 caters for a household up to six persons. Fast-boiling hot-plate, simmering-plate, two ovens and patent boiler giving enough hot water for washing-up and up to three baths daily. Overall size: 34 in. high, 34½ in. wide, 24 in. deep. In dream or cream-mottled enamel. Price £68 5*s*. Similar model without boiler (No. 30) £59 5*s*. Hire-purchase terms available. (The Esse Cooker Co., Ltd., 46 Davis Street, London, W.1.)

The 'Aga' Heat-storage Cooker and Hot-water Heater is designed for approximately the same size household and hot water requirements. Annual fuel consumption guaranteed not to exceed 3½ tons. Finished in cream vitreous enamel. Size: 34 in. high, 39 in. wide, 27 in. deep. Price £87 10*s*.; without boiler, £75. Hire-purchase terms available. (Aga Heat, Ltd., 20 North Audley Street, London, W.1.)

(*b*) THE INSULATED COOKER, also free-standing, is regulated by damper control to give the cooking temperature required. It is not so heavily insulated as the heat-storage cooker. When there is no cooking to be done, the fire burns at a low rate. This kind of cooker is on the whole less expensive than the heat-storage types, but not so economical to run. A boiler can be fitted so that the stove supplies hot water, too. A typical popular-priced example is:

The 'Rayburn' Cooker. This is designed for families up to six persons, and is continuous-burning on both coal and smokeless fuels. The water supply is sufficient for two to three baths daily. Finished in cream-mottled enamel. Size of the single-oven type: 30 in. high, 30 in. wide, 18¼ in. deep. Price £27 (without optional extras). (Allied Ironfounders, Ltd., 37–41 Mortimer Street, London, W.1.)

(*c*) THE 'COMBINATION' GRATE AND 'BACK-TO-BACK' GRATE. These are built-in, continuous-burning, multi-purpose stoves, combining an open-close fire (in the kitchen, or on the other side of the wall in a living-room) with a cooking range and hot-water boiler. They are modern in design, with easy-to-clean enamel finishes, and are a good choice for the kitchen living-room or the small home where one fire must do double duty. As cooking stoves or hot-water heaters they cannot be so efficient as the other two types mentioned above. There is, however, a wide range in size, performance and price. An example for the small family:

'*Eagle*' *B20 Combination Grate* has closed, continuous-burning fire, easily converted into open fire. The oven is placed above the hot-plate, and temperature regulated by air control in the ash-pit cover. If ducts are installed, they will give convection heating to a bedroom above. A boiler can be fitted to produce about 40 gallons of hot water a day, but the supply of hot water will depend on the position of the cylinder, whether it is lagged, and so on. Vitreous-enamel front. Overall size: 43 in. high, 20 in. wide, 14½ in. deep. Price £27 10*s*. (Eagle Range & Grate Co., Ltd., Aston, Birmingham, 6.)

Carriage, fitting costs and optional extras are not included in any of the above prices.

2. GAS COOKERS.

There is a big variety of detail in modern gas cookers, but little difference in general principle. All the new types by the various well-known makers are streamlined, easy to clean and foolproof in operation, with thermostatic oven control. Makers have aimed at getting still more economical performance, too. The usual family-size model has three or four hot-plate burners and a grill. In some models the splashback and plate-rack folds down to give a cabinet top. Cream, or cream-and-green enamel finishes instead of the usual mottled grey are available for a small extra cost. Typical examples are:

(*a*) MAIN NO. 177–14 COOKER with four-ring burners and grill. Grey-mottled vitreous enamel with black vitreous-enamel hot-plate and white flush-fitting oven door. 'Mainstat' oven heat control. Size: 36 in. high (to top of stove), 19 in. wide, 19 in. deep. Oven size: 16 in. by 13¾ in. by 12 in. Price about £20.

(*b*) RENOWN MARK 4 GAS COOKER with three boiling-burners, simmering-burner under solid plate and grill. Close-down cover fitted with folding plate-rack. Automatic hot-plate ignition. 'Adjusta' oven heat control. White vitreous-enamel finish. Size (with top cover closed): 37½ in. high, 22½ in. wide, 30½ in. deep. Oven size: 14 in. by 15 in. by 13 in. Price about £30. Fitting to point included in prices of both models. (Gas Light & Coke Co., 30 Kensington Church Street, London, W.8.)

3. ELECTRIC COOKERS.

These also vary in detail and finish, but otherwise the differences between recognised good makes are not great. Electric cookers have always been notable for their easiness to keep clean and absence of any smell of fuel. Noticeable improvements on the average pre-war models are the addition of thermostatic oven control, to all except 'baby' types, and the more flexible control of the boiling plates. Typical examples are:

(*a*) THE BELLING 'BABY' with combined grill and boiling-plate. Oven size: 13 in. by 13 in. by 11½ in. Approximate price £12 10*s*. (Belling & Co., Ltd., Bridge Works, Enfield, Middlesex.)

(*b*) SMALL REVO 'R8' with one infinitely-variable heat-controlled boiling-plate, grill-boiler, hot-cupboard. Oven size: 13¼ in. by 12¼ in. by 12½ in., thermostatically controlled.

Approximate price £22. (Revo Electric Co., Ltd., Tipton, Staffs.)

(*c*) MEDIUM-SIZE JACKSON '193 J' with one 8-in. radiant-type and one 6¼-in. enclosed-type boiling-plates, each with infinitely-variable heat control, grill-boiler and hot-cupboard. Oven size: 13½ in. by 14 in. by 12¾ in. Thermostatically controlled. Approximate price £28. (Jackson Electric Stove Co., Ltd., 143 Sloane Street, London, S.W.1.)

LAUNDRY WORK EQUIPMENT.

1. Wash-boilers and Washing Machines.

(*a*) SOLID-FUEL BOILER NO. 100 SS. Round shaped. Nominal capacity 8 gallons. Vitreous-enamel finish in grey, green or biscuit mottled enamel. Draw-off tap. Size: 28 in. high, 27 in. deep, back to front. At present available to housing schemes only. Price £15. (Carron Company, Carron, Falkirk.)

(*b*) GAS BOILER. THE 'DEAN' NO. 927A. Square shape, finished grey vitreous enamel with white-enamelled lift-off table top. Nominal capacity 8 gallons. Draw-off tap. Flue not needed. Size: 30 in. high, 19½ in. square. Price £5 11*s*. 6*d*.

(*c*) GAS-HEATED WASHING MACHINE. THE 'DEAN' NO. 928. This is an oblong-shaped wash-boiler, fitted with a hand-operated 'agitator' for washing the clothes, and an 'Acme' wringer that folds down under a white porcelain-enamel table top. Mounted on castors, it can be moved alongside the sink, provided the gas point for fitting is reasonably near. A flue need not be used. Nominal capacity 10 gallons. Size: 36¾ in. high, 19 in. wide, 22 in. deep, 14-in. roller wringer. Price £13 9*s*. 6*d*., plus purchase tax. (W. H. Dean & Son, Ltd., 200–202 Hornsey Road, London, N.7.)

(*d*) ELECTRIC WASH-BOILER. THE S.W.S. MODEL 2. Square shape, cream stove-enamel finish with vitreous-enamel table-top cover. Draw-off tap. Nominal capacity 10 gallons. Size: 30 in. high, 18 in. square. Price £12 15*s.*

(*e*) ELECTRIC HOME LAUNDRY UNIT. S.W.S. MODEL 3. This is the wash-boiler described above, with hand-operated 'agitator' for clothes washing and a detachable 'Parnall' wringlet. The latter is easily dismantled and stowed away in the bottom compartment of the machine. Price £26 19*s.* 4*d.*, inclusive of purchase tax. (South Wales Switchgear, Ltd., Blackwood, Monmouthshire.)

(*f*) MECHANICAL WASHING MACHINE, THE 'HOOVER'. A new type, with side-placed 'pulsator' which forces water currents through the clothes without direct contact with any mechanism. Designed to be filled by rubber tubing from the hot tap. Specially created for the small household and kitchen. White porcelain-enamel finish. Size: 36 in. high, 18 in. square. Price £25, plus purchase tax.

(*g*) AUTOMATIC ELECTRIC WASHING MACHINE. THE 'BENDIX' HOME LAUNDRY. This machine carries out all operations of clothes washing, from pre-soak through washing and rinsing to 'spin drying', completely automatically. Electrically operated throughout, the 'Bendix' must be connected to hot- and cold-water systems. Quite considerable plumbing work may be involved in the fixing. White porcelain-enamel top and 'baked on' enamel sides. Approximate size: 38 in. high, 26 in. wide, 23 in. deep. For A.C. mains only. Price £65, plus purchase tax. Fixing charges not included. (Bendix Home Appliances, Ltd., 99a Park Lane, London, W.1.)

2. HEATED WASH-TUB AND SINK UNIT. THE 'ROSSLOW'.

This is only suitable for house owners, as it must be built in. A double sink unit in durable enamelled fire-clay ware, with an electric sheathed element mounted at the base of the wash-tub to heat the water or boil the clothes as wanted. Wash-tub size: 24 in. by 20 in. by 14½ in. deep; with adjoining sink for rinsing, size: 24 in. by 20 in. by 10 in. deep. The detachable wringer is fixed to a galvanised-iron bearer-plate between the two sinks. Price, complete with 16-in. rubber-rollered wringer and chromium taps, £25. (Associated Clay Industries, Ltd., 3 Princes Street, Hanover Square, London, W.1.)

3. Wringers.

There is now a large selection of various kinds in shops all over the country. Typical makes are:

(*a*) THE 'PARNALL' WRINGLET. Light-weight, open-end wringer, easily adjustable pressure according to the clothes to be wrung. Can be fixed to sink, draining-board, kitchen table or a wringer stand. Weighs 12 lb. only. Enamel and chromium plated with all vulnerable parts rust proofed. Price £3 19*s.* 10½*d.*, plus purchase tax. (Parnall (Yate) Bristol, 43 Park Street, London, W.1.)

(*b*) THE 'ACME' WRINGER, a well-known and tried type. Finished cream enamel and chromium plating, with all vulnerable parts rust-proofed. 16-in. roller size, price £5 8*s.* 10*d.* including purchase tax. Also made in 14-in. size. (Acme Wringers, Ltd., David Street, Glasgow.)

4. Drying Cabinets.

(*a*) GAS HEATED. THE 'RANELAGH' DRYING AND AIRING KITCHEN CABINET. No flue normally required. The thermostatically-controlled gas unit is totally enclosed so that there is no risk of scorching. Will take 14 lb. of 'well-wrung' washing on adjustable plastic rod shelves. Consumption 30 cub. ft. per hour full on, 5 cub. ft. per hour for airing purposes. Lightweight rustless metal, cream-enamel finish. *Model* 3, size: 78 in. high, 24 in. wide, 21 in. deep. Price £26, plus purchase tax. (Ranelagh Sales Corporation, Ltd., 5 Queen Anne's Gate, London, S.W.1.)

(*b*) ELECTRICALLY-HEATED models are made by the Hotpoint Electric Appliance Co., Ltd., Crown House, Aldwych, W.C.2, and other firms. They must have a heavily loaded electric element to be capable of drying wet clothes in a fairly short time. On the other hand, *airing cabinets* only require a low loading.

The 'Elfson' Combined Cabinet Wringer is a smaller, compact piece of equipment that wrings, dries and airs clothes, and has a detachable ironing-board fixture, too. When the table-top lid is raised, the wringer is lifted into position. As the clothes are passed through the wringer, they fall on a wire grille at the back. Water is collected in a sump and run off into a bucket. Clothes are loaded on rod shelves for drying or airing. Consumption for drying, approximately 1 unit per hour. Finished in pastel-green stove enamel, with die-cast aluminium wringer stove-enamelled cream. Size: 39 in. high, 27 in. wide, 18 in. deep. Price £29. (Elfson Ltd., Tyburn Road, Birmingham, 24.)

5. IRONS.

(*a*) ELECTRIC models are now in good supply everywhere. If possible, a heat-controlled type is much to be preferred.

'Morphy-Richards' Auto-control Safety Electric Iron. A.C.: £1 15*s*.; Universal A.C./D.C.: £1 19*s*. 6*d*.

H.M.V. Heat-controlled Electric Iron. A.C.: £2 5*s*.; Universal A.C./D.C.: £2 7*s*. 6*d*.

The 'Silex' Heat-controlled Steam Iron damps while it presses, but irons dry if required. A.C. only. £3 9*s*. 6*d*.

(*b*) GAS. If electricity is not available, a gas iron, which can be run if desired on 'bottled' gas, is a great help. *The G.L.C. Gas Iron* has a simple control on the handle to allow the gas rate to be reduced to suit the type of ironing being done. £1 3*s*. 9*d*. (Gas Light & Coke Co., Ltd., 30 Kensington Church Street, London, W.8.)

6. Combined Flex-less Electric Iron and Ironing Board. (The 'Walter No Cord' Electric Iron and Board.)

Heat is obtained from a 'contact unit' on the board, which is plugged in by means of a flex to the electric point. The iron is completely free, but prongs on the iron take current from sockets on the 'contact'. The iron is thermostatically controlled, with chromium-plated finish; the board is all metal with rubber feet. The whole kit, iron included, folds up compactly for storage. A.C. only. Price complete £9 15*s*., plus £1 10*s*. 9*d*. purchase tax. (J. and H. Walter, Ltd., Domestic Appliance Division, Farm Lane, Fulham, London, S.W.6.)

7. Ironing Boards.

These are both of the standard wood and the newer, more expensive metal types, now easy to obtain from ironmongers and 'turnery' departments in stores. Some metal models have detachable sleeve board included.

ROOM-CLEANING EQUIPMENT.

Stocks are now good all over the country, so it has not been thought necessary to give makers' full name and address or specifications in any detail.

1. Carpet Sweepers.

There are many makes, and three main kinds: the standard box-shape; the rather more streamlined, flatter models; and miniature types, good for awkward corners. Prices vary largely according to detail and finish, but a reliable box-shape model can be obtained for £2 7*s*. 6*d*. and upwards, while the streamlined and miniature designs range from about £3.

2. Non-Electric Vacuum Cleaners.

These are useful where there is no electricity, or for a daily run-over instead of a carpet sweeper. Though much less powerful than the electrically-driven cleaner, this type does work with a similar suction principle, taking up embedded as well as surface dirt. The 'Newmaid', price £6 5*s*. 4*d*. The 'Whirlwind', price £5 19*s*. 6*d*.

3. Electric Vacuum Cleaners.

These are of two main types: the cylinder and the external-bag design. With the former, it is very simple to clean upholstery, curtains, wall surfaces, etc., with the one tool. On the other hand, there is a certain amount of assembling to be done each time the cleaner is used. The external-bag type, on the other hand, is immediately ready for cleaning *carpets*, but for anything else, special attachments have to be fixed. Each type has its advantages, so choice is a matter of individual preference. Examples are:

(*a*) HOOVER. Bag type. Prices: £32 16*s*. 3*d*., £26 5*s*., and £19 13*s*. 9*d*. Cylinder type, £13.

(*b*) ELECTROLUX. Cylinder type. Price £24 16*s*. 3*d*., or another model with spray, £23 10*s*. 2*d*.

(*c*) GOBLIN. Cylinder type. Prices: £12 15*s*. 11*d*., £21 13*s*. 1*d*. and £15 15*s*. Bag type, £13 15*s*. 8*d*., and £23 12*s*. 6*d* (including tools).

(*d*) ELECTRIC HAND CLEANER, for curtains, upholstery, stairs, etc. Hoover 'Dustette'. Price £7 17*s*. 6*d*.

All prices include purchase tax.

4. Electric Floor Polishers.

These will deal with tiled floors as well as parquet, linoleum and surrounds. They are almost noiseless in action and consume little current.

THE 'VACTRIC', price £23 10*s*., including purchase tax.

FOOD STORAGE EQUIPMENT.

1. Refrigerators.

These are still rather difficult to get, though the waiting time depends upon the make. There are two main types of mechanical refrigerator.

In the majority of electric models, refrigeration is effected by a motor-driven pump. Manufacturers of the motor-driven types claim that refrigeration is very much faster with their type of unit, and so ice is made in a very short time. They also say that running costs are lower and that they can provide more space inside the cabinet for the same capital outlay and floor space. Latest models of the better-known makes have the motor and compressor in a sealed container, designed to operate without attention, oiling, etc., for 20 years. Some of the post-war makes of refrigerator, though well designed, are *not* built on the 'sealed in' principle. Until new reputations have been established, care should be taken in the choice of such refrigerators. Examples of well-established makes of 'sealed in' motor-driven refrigerators are:

(*a*) THE FRIGIDAIRE. Family size, net food storage capacity 4·6 cub. ft., 36 ice cubes (4 lb. of ice) per freezing. Special frozen foods compartment, hydrator for moist storage. Automatic interior light. Size: 51¼ in. high, 26½ in. wide, 26¼ in. deep. A.C. or D.C. Price £72 10*s*., plus purchase tax.

(*b*) THE PRESTCOLD. Table-top model, net storage capacity 3·1 cub. ft., 1½ lb. of ice per freezing. Size: 36 in. high, 21½ in. wide, 23¾ in. deep. A.C. only. Price £45, plus purchase tax. Larger size, net storage capacity 4·44 cub. ft., 4 lb. of ice per freezing. Vegetable-storage compartment in base of cabinet. Automatic interior light. Price £60, plus purchase tax.

In the second type of automatic refrigerator, a motorless refrigerating unit is heat operated. This type can be *operated by gas or electricity*. Manufacturers of this type claim 'no noise, no vibration, no machinery, no working parts, no radio interference'. Well-tried examples are:

(c) ELECTROLUX MODEL LM 150 GAS OPERATED. Storage capacity 1·6 cub. ft. One small ice-cube compartment. Compact design with working-counter top. Size: 36 in. high, 21½ in. wide, 21¾ in. deep. Price £29 10*s*., plus purchase tax.

(*d*) ELECTRIC MODEL M 151, similar capacity. Suitable for 'building in'. Same price. Large model: 3 cub. ft. capacity. For gas or electricity. Price £52 10*s*., plus purchase tax.

2. VENTILATED SAFES AND STORAGE CUPBOARDS.

At a big range of prices, these are made mainly of metal, and are now in general distribution. Generally speaking, it is unwise to keep perishable food such as milk, meat, etc., in any cupboard or safe that does not have *outside* ventilation.

VENTILATION EQUIPMENT.

Two new types of electric portable units, both with very low-current consumption, for freshening the air in the kitchen or other rooms are:

1. THE 'KLEEN AIR' AIR-CONDITIONING UNIT.

This is designed to be fixed to wall or ceiling. It can be plugged in to any electrical point by a universal adaptor for plug or bayonet fitting. A silent electric fan draws the dust and fume-laden air into the grille and, after passing it through a deodoriser and chemical filter, discharges it through the side louvres back into the room, without draught. Price, coloured, £8 15*s*., including purchase tax. Chromium plated, £9 5*s*. (replacement filters 4*s*. 6*d*. each). (Appleby & Co., 6–10 Chandos House, Buckingham Gate, London, S.W.1.)

2. The Ozono Domestic Unit.

A small generator, in white cellulosed cabinet, size 7½ in. by 6 in. by 7 in. wide, can be plugged in to any electric point. Eliminates all cooking fumes. No replacements or spare parts required. Price £10 12*s*. 6*d*., including purchase tax. (E.C.D. Ltd., Tonbridge, Kent.)

KITCHEN FIXTURES.

1. The Complete 'Package Kitchen'.

This contains sink, refrigerator, cooking stove, cupboards, etc., and is not in good supply at the moment, but will probably be reintroduced. There are a few gas-kitchen models available at around £135.

2. Unit Fixtures.

Cupboards, sinks, working counters, etc., made to the British Standards Institute dimensions, are being produced by a number of firms. These are very practical, as flush fitting is obtained, whether all the units are bought at one time or later. Most of the new kitchen fixtures are of metal—steel or aluminium—with various finishes, but some wooden kitchen cabinets (not unit fixtures) are to be found. Most good department stores have a comprehensive selection at varying prices.

An example of an all-metal sink fixture is:

(*a*) 'HOUSE-PROUD' STAINLESS STEEL SINK UNIT 603. The actual sink (bowl size 20 in. by 16 in. by 8 in. deep) and draining-board are of stainless steel; the cabinet of heavy gauge, rustless aluminium, finished in cream and green stove enamel. Lined cutlery drawer on plastic roller bearings, and double cupboard. Complete with mixer taps. Overall size: 42 in. long, 21 in. wide, 36 in. high. Price £36 15*s*. (Vernons Industries Ltd., Liverpool.)

A rather more lavish unit, in solid stainless steel throughout:

(*b*) 'ELIZABETH ANN' CABINET SINK UNIT. Double sink, each bowl 21 in. by 15 in. by 8 in. deep. Swivel mixer tap; two draining-boards. Fitted five drawers and three cupboards, one with swivel tap for filling pail. Overall size: 84 in. long, 21 in. wide, 36 in. high. Price £89 5*s*., mixer valves extra. (Andrews Bros. (Bristol), Ltd., 148, Stainless House, Oldmixon, Weston-super-Mare.)

An interesting range of kitchen fitments—cookers, refrigerators, washing machines and cupboards of all kinds—is offered by the 'Udesignit' system. These can be built up according to individual requirements and the shape of the room into a flush-fitting streamlined kitchen. The finish and styling is extremely attractive. A big point is that the kitchen can be added to as means permit, while easy payment terms are offered. ('Udesignit' Patent Kitchens, in association with Weldall & Assembly, Ltd., Birmingham, 18.)

TABLE-COOKING AND MISCELLANEOUS EQUIPMENT.

THE 'ERALITE CUISINIÈRE'. A water-jacketed cooker made of fine-quality plastic and spun anodised aluminium, with a totally enclosed electric element of only 350 watts consumption. For porridge, sauces, custard, etc. Fitted 3-division egg poacher to fit in lower half. A.C. or D.C. Price £3 17*s*. 6*d*.

THE 'ERALITE CHAUDEAU.' An elegant electric kettle, for dining-room service, in bright satin silver anodised aluminium, with plastic lid and handle and insulated ball feet. Boils 3–4 pints in 6 minutes. Price £3 12*s*. 6*d*. (Eralite Manufacturing Company, Ltd., 194 The Broadway, Wimbledon, London, S.W.19.)

THE 'MOLTON' H.M.V. COFFEE PERCOLATOR. In heavily plated mirror-chrome finish, with heatproof black bakelite handle and base. No-drip spout; safety device prevents percolator boiling dry. Capacity just over 1 pint. A.C. or D.C. Price £4 17*s.* 6*d.*

THE HORIZONTAL H.M.V. ELECTRIC TOASTER. Black heat-resisting enamel body with primrose-enamelled stand and black bakelite handles. The bread is held in a plated wire frame, which takes two slices at once. The lid is enamelled inside and out, and fitted with a removable plated toast rack. Size: 3¾ in. by 6½ in. by 11½ in. A.C. or D.C. Price £4 7*s.* 6*d.* (H.M.V. Household Appliances. The Gramophone Company, Hayes, Middlesex.)

TABLE HOT-PLATE BY THE ENGLISH ELECTRIC CO., LTD. 400 watts. Price £10 10*s.* (28 Kingsway, London, W.C.2.)

Other models made by Belling & Co., Ltd., and General Electric Co.

THE 'KENWOOD' ELECTRIC FOOD MIXER. Whips eggs, batter and cream; stirs cake mixtures and cooking ingredients that need thorough mixing; mixes 'milk shakes' and similar drinks; extracts juice, and buffs cutlery and silverware. Finished cream stove enamel, with control knob and handle in black plastic, and all metal parts heavily chromium plated. Overall size: base 8 in. by 14 in., height 15 in. A.C. only. Price £17 17*s.* complete with standard attachments, plus £4 9*s.* 3*d.* purchase tax. (Woodlau Industries, Ltd., 79 Goldsworth Road, Woking, Surrey.)

PRESSURE COOKERS.

A meal in minutes, with all the goodness sealed in, is the claim of the pressure cooker. Two 'complete meal' types have been on the market for some years, and have been thoroughly tested. They are the:

1. 'EASIWORK' HEALTH COOKER. Household size No. 9. Liquid capacity 16 pints. Overall size: 17 in. high, 14 in. wide.

Price, complete with containers, £9 10*s.* (Easiwork, Ltd., 242 Tottenham Court Road, London, W.1.)

2. THE PENTECON. Model No. 5. Liquid capacity approximately 14 pints. Size: 7¼ in. high, 9½ in. diameter. Prices from £5 15*s.* 6*d.* with accessories. (Pentecon, Ltd., Hindle Street Works, Accrington, Lancs.)

A post-war type of pressure cooker, now becoming very popular, is much more of a pressure saucepan and is easier for the housewife to manipulate. A typical model with ground base, specially suitable for use with electric and solid-fuel stoves, and made of polished, drawn aluminium with black plastic handles, is the 'PRESTIGE' PRESSURE COOKER. The Hostess Model, complete with table service cover and cooking rack, £3 17*s.* 6*d.* (Platers & Stampers, Ltd., Burnley and Derby.)

Note: Prices were correct at the time of going to press, but, owing to present conditions, may have altered since.

Addresses of organisations who can give worthwhile advice on matters coming within their respective spheres are:

1. The Electrical Development Association, 2 Savoy Hill, London, W.C.2.

2. The Electrical Association for Women, 35 Grosvenor Place, London, S.W.1.

3. The British Gas Federation and the Women's Gas Council, 1 Grosvenor Place, London, S.W.1.

4. The Gas Light & Coke Co., 30 Kensington Church Street, London, W.8. (For London districts only.)

5. The Coal Utilisation Joint Council, 13 Grosvenor Gardens, London, S.W.1.

6. The Women's Advisory Council on Solid Fuel, 18 South Molton Street, London, S.W.1.

7. The Solid Smokeless Fuels Federation, 2 Grosvenor Gardens, London, S.W.1.

8. The Building Centre, 9 Conduit Street, London, W.1.

Appendix II

SOME USEFUL INFORMATION

How to Repair a Fuse.

Failure of electric light and the refusal to function of an electric appliance often means a 'blown' fuse. To replace a broken fuse, switch off current at the mains, open the fuse-box and examine the fuse-carriers, which pull out from the holders, one at a time until the carrier holding a broken wire is located. Remove the broken pieces of wire by loosening the screws which make them fast to the carrier. Wipe the carrier clean with a dry rag. Put in a new piece of fuse wire, making sure it really *is* fuse wire and of the same gauge as the broken pieces. Screw up each end without straining the new wire. Replace carrier *before* switching on at the mains. *Never* use iron or steel wire, even as a temporary measure, when repairing a fuse.

A Quick Guide to Stain Removal.

Use the simplest remedy first, and always rinse well, unless, of course, using a dry-cleaning grease solvent.

Borax or ammonia is good for all *acid* stains, e.g. fruit, wine, also tea and coffee.

A dry-cleaning grease solvent is safe for any *greasy* stain.

Commercial bleach can be used cautiously on white cottons or household linen, but use only as a last resource.

Go carefully with *oxalic acid* (at present this is very difficult to obtain), which is poisonous and corrosive.

When using *permanganate of potash*, make up a very mild solution, or the remedy may be worse than the cure.

Tea, coffee, cocoa, fruit, vegetables, wine, vinegar.	Leave to soak in a warm borax or ammonia solution (1 teaspoonful of borax, 1 tablespoonful of household ammonia to ½ pint of water). If you don't want to get the whole article wet, stretch the stained part over a bowl, sprinkle on borax and pour hot water through. With a non-washable fabric, sponge carefully with a borax solution and pat as dry as possible. Stains must be treated when fresh. For obstinate stains on cotton or linen use a commercial bleach (e.g. Parozone) according to directions.
Egg, milk.	Sponge with warm water. When dry, use a dry-cleaning grease solvent.
Fat, grease or oil.	Sponge with a cloth dipped in dry-cleaning grease solvent.
Blood.	Steep in cold salt water.
Perspiration.	Very difficult to remove. Try soaking in a warm borax solution. Then wash in the ordinary way.
Paint.	Sponge with a cloth dipped in turps substitute.
Ink (writing).	When the fabric will not be injured by boiling water, stretch over a basin, sprinkle with a few oxalic acid crystals and pour the water through. Otherwise make up a little permanganate of potash in the proportion of ¼ teaspoonful of crystals to a teacup of warm water.

	Drop a teaspoonful of the solution on to the inkstain and after a minute rinse away. Then treat in the same way using 10 vol. peroxide diluted with four times the amount of warm water. Milk will take out some of the stain left by newly spilled ink, but won't remove it altogether.
Ink (marking).	Try the permanganate and peroxide method.
Ink (red).	Soaking in a borax and water solution may do the trick. If not, dab on a touch of methylated spirits.
Scorch marks.	Difficult to remove, but soapy warm water well softened with borax may work. Try rubbing a little 'neat' borax on the mark and then gently wash through.
Laundry blue.	Dip in weak vinegar and water (dessertspoonful of vinegar to ½ pint of water).
Iron mould.	Treat with oxalic acid as for writing ink.
Scent, water or heat marks on polished furniture.	Make a pad of cotton wool. Pour on a few drops of methylated spirits, cover with two thicknesses of butter muslin. Work in a circular motion over the mark, the aim being to remove just enough stain from the surrounding wood to mask the bare ring.

A QUICK GUIDE TO APPROXIMATE 'COOKING MEASURES'.

Flour, cornflour, cocoa, custard powder.	1 level tablespoonful	½ oz.
	1 heaped tablespoonful	1 oz.
	1 good teacupful	a bare 4 oz.

Sugar and 'heavy' cereals, also golden syrup.	1 level tablespoonful	1 oz.
	1 bare teacupful	6 ozs.
Fat.	1 tablespoonful	1 oz.
	piece size of hen's egg	1 oz.
Liquids.	1 teacupful	⅓ pt.
	1 big breakfastcupful	½ pt.

A Quick Guide to Oven Settings.

Slow oven	275°–325°	(Fahrenheit)	Regulo 1–2
Moderate oven	325°–375°	,,	Regulo 2–4
Moderately hot oven	375°–425°	,,	Regulo 4–6
Hot oven	425°–475°	,,	Regulo 6–8
Very hot oven	475°–500°	,,	Regulo 8–10

Electric ovens are usually marked in degrees, or if in figures 1 equals 100° F., and so on. Gas ovens have different settings according to make. A rough guide is that the lowest setting (Regulo ¼, Mainstat A or 2, Parkinson Thermostat 1, Flavel Thermostat B, New Herald Thermostat 1, New Home Autokook ½–1, Cannon Autimo 1) approximates to 250° F., and that each setting goes up by about 25° F. It's a good plan to get exact temperature equivalents in degrees for the settings on your make of oven, and make a chart to pin near the cooker. Then it's easy to 'translate' recipes.

INDEX

If you have enjoyed this Persephone book why not telephone or write to us for a free copy of the *Persephone Catalogue* and the current *Persephone Biannually*? All Persephone books ordered from us cost £12 or three for £30 plus £2 postage per book.

PERSEPHONE BOOKS LTD
59 Lamb's Conduit Street
London WC1N 3NB

Telephone: 020 7242 9292
sales@persephonebooks.co.uk
www.persephonebooks.co.uk